BIRDHOUSES

of the **WORLD**

TO DAWN GRABER AND
OUR DAUGHTER, MARY SCHMAUSS.

BIRDHOUSES
of the WORLD

ANNE SCHMAUSS

STEWART, TABORI & CHANG | NEW YORK

PREVIOUS SPREAD: BIRDHOUSES AT THE EDGE OF A SALT MARSH ON CAPE COD IN SANDWICH, MASSACHUSETTS.

RIGHT: OWLS LIKE THIS EASTERN SCREECH OWL ARE HAPPY TO USE A BIRDHOUSE.

OPPOSITE: A MALE WOOD DUCK SITS ATOP HIS HOUSE.

OVERLEAF: AN ART INSTALLATION COMPRISED OF BIRDHOUSES NEAR TOLYATTI CITY IN RUSSIA.

TABLE *of* CONTENTS

THIS PURPLE MARTIN HOUSE IS A MODERN VERSION OF THE GOURDS USED BY NATIVE AMERICANS.

CHICKADEES, INCLUDING THIS CAROLINA CHICKADEE, ARE CAVITY NESTERS AND WILL READILY COME TO BIRDHOUSES.

INTRODUCTION

While I was writing *Birdhouses of the World*, so many people told me they had a neighbor or an uncle who built birdhouses. It turns out that building birdhouses is a very common hobby, especially in the United States and Canada. I shouldn't have been surprised, as I've owned a Wild Birds Unlimited store since 1994 and know firsthand how popular birdhouses are. I've sold thousands of birdhouses and had just as many conversations about them. The variety of birdhouses available today is staggering. No longer are birdhouses merely functional nest boxes for birds; now, many are art objects, while others are intended as conversation pieces or perhaps even as commentary on the state of our environment (as you'll see in the Trash Tree from Denmark and the projects by London Fieldworks).

For this book my goal was simply to find the coolest birdhouses on the planet and tell their stories. And what stories they have! In Japan, I found a massive bird apartment that was as much art installation as birdhouse; in Oregon, I found Layla Coats, who meticulously crafts lovely birdhouses from river stones; in Delaware, I found Thomas Burke, who built a monumental replica of George Lucas's Skywalker Ranch.

That birdhouse is installed at the real Skywalker Ranch today. I hope you'll find something appealing about each birdhouse and perhaps you might fall in love with the birdhouse creators as much as I did.

A BRIEF HISTORY

The first structures built by humans for birds were specifically for pigeons and doves and are commonly known as dovecotes. Pigeons were among the earliest domesticated livestock, going back almost ten thousand years, and old dovecotes, some of them thousands of years old, can still be found all over the world and in almost every culture. Throughout history, these dovecotes have been used primarily to raise pigeons and doves for the dinner table (meat and eggs) and as a source of fertilizer for crops and gardens. In the Middle Ages, particularly in France, a dovecote was a sign of great wealth and status. Although the design of dovecotes varies throughout history and from culture to culture, most are somewhat dome shaped (or cylindrical) and hollow in the middle, and most have perches for the birds on the inside and sometimes even on the outside. They were often quite large—in Europe, they could be as tall as

a small building or tower—with smooth walls on the outside to keep predators from climbing up and into the house. The dung that was used as fertilizer collected on the ground underneath the perches inside the house for easy gathering.

Dovecotes in ancient Egypt were, and still are, constructed out of mud brick so that they can withstand the desert heat and wind. In his book *Earth Architecture*, Ronald Rael refers to the widespread use of dovecotes throughout Egypt: "In a country with little arable land, the bizarre dovecotes are a crucial part of urban planning and feeding a nation of eighty million people."

Birdhouses, unlike dovecotes, were created to provide a home and a safe haven for wild birds and their families. Birdhouses haven't been around as long as dovecotes, but they seemed to have appeared several hundred years ago in many cultures around the world.

As early as the fifteenth century and on through the nineteenth century, the Turks were incorporating birdhouses into the facades of many structures, including mosques, libraries, churches, and bridges. The birdhouse shown on pages 14–15 is a lovely example of delicate workmanship on the Ayazma Mosque, which was built in the 1760s, in the Üsküdar district of

THIS BIRDHOUSE IS BUILT INTO
THE FAÇADE OF AN EIGHTEENTH-
CENTURY MOSQUE IN ISTANBUL,
TURKEY, AND IS STILL BEING
USED BY BIRDS.

Istanbul, Turkey. The keeper of the Ayazma Mosque also takes care of its birdhouses. He carefully cleans out the birdhouses so they are ready for new nesters. It's impressive to me that, after all this time, someone still maintains these birdhouses. Turkey has some fine examples of dovecotes dating back to ancient times, but according to the Turkish Cultural Foundation, birdhouses are the true symbol of the value and importance Turks place on animals, especially birds.

In Europe both dovecotes and birdhouses have been common since the fifteenth century. For much of that time, however, the birdhouses functioned more as traps than as safe homes for the birds, for they gave birdhouse keepers easy access to the eggs and young birds for food.

For hundreds of years, Native Americans have been using the simplest of birdhouses made from hollowed-out gourds. These were designed for birds like purple martins, which are voracious flying-insect eaters and are a tremendous help in keeping the insect population down wherever they live. European settlers adopted this practice as a natural insect-control measure for their yards, gardens, and fields. In the mid- to late nineteenth century and into the twentieth century, large, ornate wooden martin houses became widespread. Smaller birdhouses for wrens, chickadees, and other birds also became popular in the United States during this period.

WHICH BIRDS USE BIRDHOUSES?

While the vast majority of bird species do not use birdhouses, nearly eighty species of birds in North America do. These birds are cavity nesters—birds that typically use hollow cavities inside living or dead tree trunks as nesting sites. Often these cavities were originally created by woodpeckers and later taken over by other species. Birdhouses, often called nest boxes, simply take the place of a natural cavity for these birds. Cavity nesters include woodpeckers, chickadees, nuthatches, flycatchers, owls, and wrens. (For a more detailed list, see the chart on pages 128–29.) Birds that don't use birdhouses build their nests elsewhere. This includes birds like robins, cardinals, and hummingbirds, who build their nests on the branches of trees or in shrubs, as well as other birds, like towhees, juncos, and killdeer, who build their nests on the ground.

LEFT: THIS DOVECOTE IS IN THE SINAI DESERT IN EGYPT, BUT MANY MORE JUST LIKE IT ARE FOUND THROUGHOUT EGYPT.

RIGHT: THIS CHARMING STONE DOVECOTE (CALLED A *DOOCOT* IN SCOTLAND) STANDS ON THE GROUNDS OF THE SIXTEENTH-CENTURY CRATHES CASTLE IN THE ABERDEENSHIRE REGION OF SCOTLAND.

SKYWALKER RANCH BIRDHOUSE

WHEN THOMAS BURKE, OWNER OF THOMAS BURKE FINE BIRDHOMES, FIRST READ THE E-MAIL FROM MELLODY ASKING IF HE WOULD BUILD A BIRDHOUSE FOR HER BOYFRIEND, GEORGE, HE DIDN'T TAKE IT TOO SERIOUSLY. It took a bit of back and forth before he realized that Mellody was Mellody Hobson, president of Ariel Investments, a Chicago-based investment firm, and at the time a financial news contributor for *Good Morning America*. And her boyfriend? George Lucas, of *Star Wars* fame.

According to Burke, Hobson and Lucas had seen his work in a magazine and liked it so much that Hobson commissioned a project: a replica of the 50,000-square-foot main house on Lucas's Skywalker Ranch in Marin County, California. Blueprints of the ranch were mailed to Burke in Delaware, and he began working on the massive, luxury birdhome (the word *birdhouse* doesn't seem grand enough). After four months, the replica was finished. In April 2011, after a trip cross-country in a truck, the house was installed at the real Skywalker Ranch.

The birdhouse is roughly the size of a Volkswagen Beetle convertible and has four levels with fifty individual compartments, each with its own bird entry port made from PVC piping. Most of the materials used in its construction were recycled.

Burke is accustomed to building large birdhouses patterned after beautiful homes, but the Skywalker Ranch house is his biggest

Birdhouse Details

MOST LIKELY INHABITANTS: sparrows, European starlings

DIMENSIONS: 9' w x 3' h x 5' d

WEIGHT: 600 lbs.

The birdhouse features four levels with fifty individual compartments, each with a bird entry port made from PVC piping. It was constructed from recycled/reused materials, including seven sheets of plywood, and five wooden shipping crates, which were cut down and used to make the roof and clapboard siding. The house was built, shipped, and installed in three sections and took four men and a forklift to install.

OPPOSITE: THE BIRDHOUSE ON GEORGE LUCAS'S SKYWALKER RANCH IS ABOUT THE SIZE OF A SMALL CAR.

THOMAS BURKE WORKED METICULOUSLY IN HIS GARAGE FOR ABOUT FOUR MONTHS BUILDING
THE SKYWALKER RANCH BIRDHOUSE.

HEAVY MACHINERY AND SEVERAL MEN WERE REQUIRED TO INSTALL THE SIX-HUNDRED-POUND BIRDHOUSE.

to date. He turned to furniture making in the early 2000s after spending years in the custom-home-building business. After a friend asked him to build a birdhouse patterned on her home, he discovered he was pretty good at it and shifted his focus to building more. Soon, word spread, and Thomas was being asked to build birdhouses for the owners of fine homes throughout the northeast.

Burke has long admired the paintings of artist Andrew Wyeth, so much so that more than a dozen of his birdhouses have been inspired by buildings in Wyeth's paintings. Wyeth himself was so impressed by Burke's artistry that in 2009, he and his wife commissioned Burke to build a birdhouse as a gift for their son Jamie. Having won such a seal of approval from an icon of American art is one of Burke's proudest achievements.

After Burke's birdhouses were featured in a June 2010 spread in *Architectural Digest*, business began to boom. It was this article that had caught Mellody Hobson's eye. Some of Burke's birdhouses line the riverwalk in his hometown of Wilmington. He's built more than a hundred birdhouses, and sells them for an average of $6,500 apiece. "Many have sold for more than ten thousand dollars," says Burke. Economic uncertainty in recent years hasn't hurt Burke's business one bit. "It's the wealthy who buy what I make, and the wealthy are still wealthy!" he says.

Architectural Digest called Burke "America's birdhouse designer-builder extraordinaire." The birdhouse he built for Hobson and Lucas is certainly proof that Burke takes that label seriously. (By the way, he still has that first e-mail from Mellody Hobson.)

Birdhouse Details

MOST LIKELY INHABITANTS:
purple martins, sparrows,
European starlings

DIMENSIONS:
46" w x 44" h x 34" d

WEIGHT: 225 lbs.

Burke used old wooden shipping
crates for all of the wood,
including the roof shingles, which
he cut to look like cedar shake
shingles. The roof can be removed
for cleaning. The home is fitted
with gutters, downspouts, and
ten copper lightning rods, as
well as eight dormers and upper
sashes in all of the windows

A COPPER PORCH ROOF IS ONE OF THE MANY DETAILS BURKE INCLUDED
IN THE CANTITOE CORNERS BIRDHOUSE. THE REAL HOUSE DOES NOT
HAVE A COPPER ROOF; BURKE JUST LIKED HOW IT LOOKED.

CANTITOE CORNERS BIRDHOUSE

In addition to his replica of Skywalker Ranch, Thomas Burke has built a birdhouse patterned after Cantitoe Corners, Martha Stewart's home in Bedford, New York. (The project was not commissioned by Stewart; Burke constructed it of his own volition, using existing photographs of the property.)

According to a September 10, 2006, *New York Times* article and the *Martha Moments* blog, Cantitoe Corners is a 153-acre compound comprised of seven structures, including a main house that was built in 1925. Stewart purchased the property in 2000 and named the property after Cantitoe, the wife of Katonah, a Ramapough Indian chief who lived in the area in the late seventeenth century. The main house served as the model for Burke's birdhouse.

Burke spent almost two years, on and off, working on the birdhouse, which is constructed entirely of recycled materials.

As part of his homage to Stewart, he used only Martha Stewart branded paint for this project—mostly Bedford Gray. Before he began to paint the birdhouse, Burke opened the new paint cans and let them sit, uncovered, overnight, causing the paint to thicken. As a result, when he applied a few coats to the surface of the birdhouse, it looked like many coats of paint applied over many years.

The chimney was first built of wood then covered with concrete patch. While it was still soft, Burke cut shapes in the concrete with a razor knife to look like bricks and stones. He then applied four to five coats of paint to re-create the look of different colored stones.

BURKE PATTERNED THIS BIRDHOUSE AFTER MARTHA STEWART'S CANTITOE CORNERS HOME.

He used the same technique for the stonework in the lower-front part of the house. Burke covered the porch roof with copper, a detail it does not share with Stewart's house.

Birdhouse makers sometimes construct individual entry ports that lead into one large internal compartment, which isn't ideal for the birds. Burke goes to the considerable trouble and extra expense to create a cavity for each bird. This replica features twenty-eight lined bird-entry ports, each with an individual interior compartment.

The Cantitoe Corners birdhouse can be seen along the Wilmington, Delaware, riverwalk alongside fifteen other Thomas Burke birdhouses.

WHILE RESEARCHING THIS BOOK, I WAS SURPRISED BY HOW FEW WOMEN I FOUND MAKING INCREDIBLE BIRDHOUSES. However, I hit the jackpot with Layla Coats. This young woman is an artist, but in 2008, her art took a detour. One day, while sitting on her front porch in Washington, she noticed for the first time how loud the birds were. "They sounded like they were wearing microphones," Coats remembers. "They started shouting at me." This was all the inspiration she needed—and she's been building birdhouses ever since.

Coats loves wine and had saved the corks from open bottles with the thought that someday she'd find a way to incorporate them into her art. She discovered a way when she started making birdhouses. She cuts each cork in half so it lies flat against the walls of the birdhouse. These days Coats can't drink enough wine to fuel her birdhouse business, so friends contribute their corks, too.

Most materials found in Coats's birdhouses are objects she gathers on her travels. Her husband is a bridge builder, and she usually likes to go with him when he travels on business. Their adventures take them all over the Pacific Northwest. While her husband is busy working on-site, usually right on a river, Coats spends hours picking rocks along the shorelines. She has found an amazing variety of rocks throughout the region. A typical Winestone Birdhouse might include coastal agates from southern Oregon or fool's gold from Leavenworth, Washington, or maybe even an actual obsidian arrowhead. On walks with her dog, Coats gathers all sorts of goodies for her birdhouses, like little sticks for birdhouse perches and any rocks she finds appealing. She always carries a plastic bag in her pocket to stash her finds.

Coats builds her houses assembly-line style. She lines up the birdhouse shells and then stains and lacquers the roof of each one. After choosing a perch for each house, she decides on their individual themes, filling trays with the different building materials that she will incorporate. This may include rocks, corks, bullet casings, beads, and whatever else Coats decides for a particular house. Using tweezers and a hot glue gun, she slowly and carefully pieces together each unique birdhouse. On a birdhouse featuring bullet casings, for example, she might also glue on a miniature replica of a pistol.

Most people who buy Winestone Birdhouses prize them as works of art and keep them indoors. Coats's birdhouses don't have drainage holes and can't easily be cleaned, so they're probably best used as decorative pieces.

COATS LINES UP THE MATERIALS SHE PLANS TO USE FOR A PARTICULAR BIRDHOUSE IN SEPARATE TRAYS. THE TWEEZERS AND ASSEMBLY OF VERY SMALL ITEMS SHOW THE FINE DETAIL WORK REQUIRED.

THIS PHOTO WAS TAKEN ALONG THE DESCHUTES RIVER, SOUTH OF SUNRIVER, OREGON, IN THE CENTRAL PART OF THE STATE, WHERE LAYLA LIVES. THESE SEVEN BIRDHOUSES REPRESENT A VARIETY OF LAYLA'S WORK. COATS OFTEN GOES SHOOTING WITH HER FATHER, WHICH EXPLAINS HER STEADY SUPPLY OF RECYCLED BULLET SHELLS (SEE THE SECOND

 Birdhouse Details (see above, left to right)

1) DIMENSIONS:
7" w x 9" h x 7" d

MATERIALS:
- Polished, colorful stones including coastal agates from the Oregon coast
- Textured river rocks from Leavenworth, Washington
- Black obsidian from central Oregon
- Purple flower charm with amethyst and bronze embellishments
- Bronze "Made with Love" tag

2) DIMENSIONS:
6" w x 8½" h x 6½" d

MATERIALS:
- Bullet shell casings, wood rounds, and wine corks
- Coastal agates, Oregon lava rocks
- A small fake revolver and black bear detail on the front
- Layla calls this her Man's Birdhouse.

3) AND 5) DIMENSIONS:
2½" w x 4" h x 4" d

MATERIALS:
- Entrance hole: black and pink glass beads (3); lighter glass beads (5)
- Green and pink gemstones, as well as river rocks and colorful agates

BIRDHOUSE FROM THE LEFT). SHE FIRST INCORPORATED BULLET SHELLS INTO A BIRDHOUSE SHE MADE FOR HER FATHER, AND IT HAS SINCE BECOME ONE OF THE MOST POPULAR BIRDHOUSE FEATURES.

4) DIMENSIONS:
6½" w x 8½" h x 6½" d

MATERIALS:
- Entrance holes: rustic metal stars
- Layered roof finished in walnut varnish
- Wine corks, wood rounds, and twigs
- Coastal agates and beads

6) DIMENSIONS:
6" w x 8½" h x 6½" d

MATERIALS:
- Entrance hole: pearl white and glass beads
- Bronze love-dove metal disc on the front
- Colorful Pacific Ocean agates and amethyst stones
- Layla calls this the King Estate Birdhouse.

7) DIMENSIONS:
9" w x 13" h x 7" d

MATERIALS:
- Polished gemstones and coastal agates from southern Oregon
- Textured river rocks
- Rough lava from Deschutes National Forest
- Tiny silver icons of birds in flight
- Small silver frame containing an image of a little yellow bird

Birdhouse Details

MOST LIKELY INHABITANTS: woodpeckers, nuthatches, chickadees, wrens, sparrows

DIMENSIONS: 12" w x 35" h (with mounting bracket)

WEIGHT: 25 lbs.

ENTRANCE HOLE: 2½" x 2"

The welded steel roof is ⅛" thick

OPPOSITE: CATEAUX, WEARING HIS BLACKSMITHING APRON, STANDS NEXT TO HIS ONE-OF-A-KIND BIRDHOUSE.

ANTHONY CATEAUX WAS BORN IN IRELAND BUT NOW LIVES ON VANCOUVER ISLAND IN BRITISH COLUMBIA. His one-of-a-kind birdhouse was inspired by the Edvard Munch painting *The Scream*, though we can't give Munch full credit since the work of a woodpecker also served as inspiration for Cateaux.

After cutting down a dead tree in 2012 on his forested property outside of Ladysmith, British Columbia, Cateaux noticed that a woodpecker had been using part of the trunk as a nesting site. The bird had pecked out a good-size entrance hole and then stumbled upon a four-inch wide cavity that ran all the way through a section of the log from top to bottom. The hidden, hollow vertical core of the dead tree must have been the perfect nesting spot. Feeling the need to replace the natural birdhouse he had just cut down, Cateaux applied his talent and skill toward turning this log into a special birdhouse.

Cateaux calls himself an "artist smith." He apprenticed as a blacksmith for six years in Toronto and has worked for many years crafting high-end custom-made metal furniture and other one-of-a-kind art pieces. It was only natural that he would use metal in his birdhouse.

Before getting started on the project, Cateaux used tracing paper to make a template from the face of the log, which he then used to transfer the image to metal. He constructed the face from several different pieces of metal and welded them together. Some of the natural breaks in the face of the birdhouse are where the pieces are connected.

A CLOSE-UP OF THE HAND-FORGED FACE AND BLUE EYES. VANCOUVER ISLAND IS A RAINY PLACE.

To make the hands, Cateaux traced his own hands onto a sheet of copper with a scribe. Then, using heavy-duty metal shears, he cut the hands out of the copper sheet. Cateaux placed the copper hands into his forge to soften them, then added the details using a hammer, small chisel, and scribe. Look closely to see fingernails, knuckles, and other details etched in the copper. The eyes were added with metallic blue paint.

Cateaux forged all of the metal used for the birdhouse in his own metal forge. The heat of the forge softens the metal, making it easier to manipulate, and gives it a rich, dark patina. The top-to-bottom vertical core of the birdhouse made it necessary for Cateaux to construct a floor for the structure from a metal plate. He sealed the outside of the piece with wax to help offset the effects of Vancouver Island's rainy climate. The metal roof is pitched to keep out the frequent rain and to help keep baby birds dry. Hammered copper cups attached to the roof are designed to catch the rain, which in turn gives the copper a nice green patina. Cateaux also crafted and forged the heavy-duty brackets that are used for mounting the birdhouse.

THE SCREAM BIRDHOUSE TOOK ANTHONY CATEAUX ALMOST TWO WEEKS TO BUILD AND WEIGHS MORE THAN TWENTY-FIVE POUNDS. CHECK OUT THE DETAIL ON THE COPPER HANDS.

Birdhouse Details

Double-bell Birdhouse

MOST LIKELY INHABITANTS:
wrens, chickadees, sparrows

DIMENSIONS: approximately
4½' h; 12" x 12" base

WEIGHT: 32 lbs.

ENTRANCE HOLE: 1½" diameter

The roof is made of vintage tin ceiling tiles, and the birdhouse features a vintage doorknob and doorplate, crosses, bells, and spindles.

LORENZO PADILLA HAS WORKED HARD FOR MORE THAN TWENTY YEARS TO FULFILL HIS DREAM OF TURNING HIS BIRDHOUSES INTO A SUCCESSFUL BUSINESS. He works every day—except Christmas—loading his truck with his colorful birdhouses and driving across the United States from art show to art show to sell them. Padilla, who immigrated decades ago with his parents to Houston, Texas, by way of Honduras and Mexico, has been in Texas for so long that he feels "like a real Texan."

Architecture has been Padilla's passion since he was a kid, when his dad taught him carpentry. But his parents couldn't afford architecture school so he became an accountant to make a living. In the early 1990s, inspired by the French Quarter architecture he saw in New Orleans, Padilla started building birdhouses as a hobby. His combination of tireless effort and creativity has paid off. Now it's a full-time endeavor, and at art shows, he often sells hundreds of birdhouses in a single weekend. He has a seven-person crew in his shop in Houston, and his parents also help out. Now in their seventies, they mix the custom paints and stains he uses on his birdhouses; they also travel cross-country with him to most of the art shows he attends.

Padilla is particularly proud that all of his birdhouses are built by hand, as well as the fact that he uses recycled, salvaged materials. All of the doorknobs, doorplates, grate pieces, furniture spindles, and wood are salvaged materials. He and his crew drive around Houston looking for wood and remodeling castoffs. Old wood siding is a great find—sometimes they stumble upon pieces dating as far back as the nineteenth century. Hundred-year-old tin ceiling tiles

OPPOSITE: THIS RED DOUBLE-BELL BIRDHOUSE IS ONE OF PADILLA'S MOST POPULAR DESIGNS.

LORENZO PADILLA'S COLORFUL CREATIONS.

are used to make roofs. The spindles come from old staircases, beds, chairs, and other furniture. Scouring the city for the old doorknobs and other vintage decorative pieces has become quite a time-consuming venture, so now this task is done by others.

Padilla's birdhouses are always evolving. Although his first birdhouses were small, some of his current models are five feet tall. The size, color, shape, and architectural elements are in constant flux, and no two houses are alike. Probably the most distinguishing feature of his birdhouses is their bright, vivid colors.

His goal is to create unique, fairly priced birdhouses that will delight his customers. One extremely happy customer in Atlanta owns several *dozen* of Padilla's birdhouses. He estimates that seventy percent of his customers choose to keep his birdhouses inside their homes as artwork (the middle of the dining room table seems to be a popular spot to display them).

OPPOSITE: THIS SINGLE-BELL HOUSE IS ONE OF MY FAVORITES.

WHEN I STUMBLED UPON THE IMAGES OF LONDON FIELDWORKS BIRDHOUSES IN MY RESEARCH FOR THIS BOOK, I WAS BLOWN AWAY. Based in East London, London Fieldworks was formed in 2000 by artists Bruce Gilchrist and Jo Joelson as a collaborative arts practice. They have completed art works around the world, including projects in Brazil, Scotland, Norway, and England. They decided on birdhouses as one expression of their art and as a commentary on what they call "dwindling biodiversity and population crashes in nature." Although they look nothing like any birdhouse you've ever seen, these works have nonetheless become homes for birds like great tits and wood pigeons. Birdhouses they may be, but they sit at the intersection of art, science, and nature.

King's Wood is an ancient woodland site in Kent, England, and is home to several of London Fieldworks's birdhouse structures. In the Middle Ages, this forest was part of the king's personal hunting grounds, but is now open to the public. According to Gilchrist and Joelson, both the Mussolini and Ceausescu installations in King's Wood were "based on the palaces of despots to reflect the destructive forces in human societies." Both structures are part of a project they call Super Kingdom, built in 2008. The works were commissioned by Stour Valley Arts.

Like so many places in recent years, the landscape around Kent is being swallowed up by encroaching development. London Fieldworks's projects are a response to that loss of green space, and the

THE SPONTANEOUS CITY BIRDHOUSE IS LOCATED IN THE ST. JAMES CHURCH GARDEN IN THE DISTRICT OF CLERKENWELL, LONDON.

Birdhouse Details

Spontaneous City
MOST LIKELY INHABITANTS: great tits, robins

DIMENSIONS: 10' h

Commissioned by Clerkenwell Design Week and constructed from untreated spruce. The birdhouse is attached to an expanding rubber corset.

Mussolini (page 40)
MOST LIKELY INHABITANTS: great tits, wood pigeons

DIMENSIONS: 10½' h

Commissioned by Stour Valley Arts and constructed from an assembly of units made from untreated spruce ply.

Ceausescu (page 41)
MOST LIKELY INHABITANTS: wood pigeons

DIMENSIONS: 12' h

Commissioned by Stour Valley Arts and constructed from galvanized steel.

loss of habitat for birds and animals. The birdhouses are designed to provoke speculation and thought about these issues, forcing us to ask questions and perhaps even find some of the answers: "Is it conservation? Maybe it's art? Might something live there? How can something live in art?" But that is Gilchrist and Joelson's intention: They want people to wonder about these birdhouses, to question them, to try to figure them out.

It can take many weeks to plan, design, build, and install each of these structures. Installation alone can take five days. Before designing and building each project, the artists and team at London Fieldworks hire a tree surgeon to survey and measure the tree. They then make a 3-D representation of the tree and map their design onto it. A crew of artists and carpenters build the birdhouse unit and attach it to an expanding rubber corset wrapped around the tree. This allows the birdhouse structure to expand as the tree grows, leaving both unharmed. Cherry pickers or scaffolding towers are used to aid installation.

Several of these amazing works can be seen by anyone who visits King's Wood and walks the beautiful paths through the forest. Gilchrist and Joelson say "there have been no official complaints, and so far the work hasn't been vandalized, except by gray squirrels."

OPPOSITE: THIS ONE IS PATTERNED AFTER NICOLAE CEAUSESCU'S PALACE IN BUCHAREST, ROMANIA.

Birdhouse Details

(Applies to most Shuping birdhouses)

MOST LIKELY INHABITANTS:
wrens, chickadees, bluebirds

DIMENSIONS:
6" diameter x 24" h (some are as tall as 29"); 4" finials;
4" to 14" bottom spindles

WEIGHT: 4 lbs.

ENTRANCE HOLES: 1¼" or 1½" diameter

Typical woods used are walnut, maple, and cherry.

OPPOSITE: THESE EASTERN BLUEBIRDS SEEM INTERESTED IN THIS WOOD-TURNED BIRDHOUSE.

WOODWORKING EQUIPMENT IS RARELY THE INSPIRATION FOR ART, BUT BOB SHUPING POINTS TO GETTING A WOOD LATHE IN 1998 AS THE INSPIRATION FOR HIS WOOD-TURNED BIRDHOUSES. A native of North Carolina, Shuping had worked as a custom-home builder since the mid-1980s. But by the late 1990s, Shuping said, "It got so that I was driving around in my truck all day checking on my building crews." His connection to the art of woodworking, which had always been central to his home-building business, was slipping away.

Enter the wood lathe. His creative spark reignited, Shuping soon found himself spending more time in his woodshop working with the lathe to create unique wood pieces, including birdhouses. That first year, he gave his birdhouses as Christmas presents to friends and family, and by spring was hearing all sorts of stories of happy birds nesting in his homes. "Building birdhouses is the best minimum-wage job I've ever had," he says. And according to Shuping, building his unique birdhouses allows him to "use almost every aspect of wood turning."

He focuses on the kind of wood he's working with, noticing the different grains, textures, patterns, and colors. Shuping air-dries each board for a very long period of time, sometimes even years. Unlike kiln-drying, air-drying is a very slow process but yields a more dramatic-looking wood. According to Shuping, air-drying makes the wood stronger and brings out more color and contrast. To air-dry his lumber, Shuping lays out each board, stacking one on top of the other with a spacer in between so that air can flow all around the wood. If he's making a custom birdhouse, he lets the customer wander the stacks looking for just the right boards, with just the

BOB SHUPING WITH HIS WORKS IN PROGRESS. WHAT A BEAUTIFUL VIEW SHUPING HAS TO LOOK UPON AS HE BUILDS HIS BEAUTIFUL BIRDHOUSES!

right pattern. This close attention to raw materials is indicative of Shuping's attention to detail and craft.

Shuping also talks about how woodworking has brought him closer to the trees. Hurricane Fran brought severe storms to North Carolina in 1996, downing some old walnut trees on a friend's land. He bought those trees and is still using the wood they provided. During a fierce 2003 ice storm, Shuping harvested red maple, hickory, holly, and pear trees that otherwise would have died and gone to rot. He loves discovering red maple trees lying on the forest floor. Red maples have high sugar content, which at-

tracts ambrosia beetles. When ambrosia beetles feast on red maples, they introduce a fungus that causes beautiful and dramatic colors and patterns in the wood. This fungus does not harm the integrity of the wood—it simply enhances its natural beauty, especially when that wood finds its way into the hands of a master like Shuping.

OPPOSITE: THE BODY OF THIS BIRDHOUSE IS MADE OF RED MAPLE AND FEATURES DEEP COLORED GRAIN CRAFTED WITH THE HELP OF THE AMBROSIA BEETLE. SHUPING'S FINE CRAFTSMANSHIP AND LOVE OF WOOD WERE ALSO IMPORTANT FACTORS IN GETTING THE LOOK OF THIS BIRDHOUSE JUST RIGHT.

DAVID BRUCE IS A TRUE ARIZONA MAVERICK. Twenty years ago, inspired by the trees in his Phoenix backyard and the color of the wildflowers growing there, Bruce built a birdhouse. When an acquaintance, who owned an antique store, saw Bruce's creation, he asked Bruce to build a few birdhouses for his shop. He sold fifteen the first week. Bruce loved building birdhouses so much that he decided to quit his job and make birdhouses full time. Two weeks after making his *first* birdhouse, he was making them for a living. And he has never looked back.

In the early years, Bruce couldn't afford new wood, so he used what he found on the street or in the trash. He preferred the look of the old stuff anyway. At first he used his buck knife to cut the old wood, but later he was able to buy a saw. Money was so tight in the beginning that Bruce sometimes collected bent nails and straightened them to use in his birdhouses.

To broaden his customer base, Bruce had to go out and hustle. He would build houses all week long, and on the weekends he'd load up his '68 Buick and drive from shop to shop, town to town, state to state, until he sold them all. Then he'd do it all over again the next week. It took an awful lot of commitment on his part, but eventually his persistence paid off. Today, David Bruce's Weathered Wonders birdhouses are sold in more than 130 shops and art galleries across the country. A Phoenix, Arizona, magazine named Bruce one of the city's most successful businesspeople, although that label embarrasses him: "It's like when people call me an 'artist.' I make birdhouses out of junk," says Bruce. "I'm not da Vinci!"

Birdhouse Details

MOST LIKELY INHABITANTS:
wrens, chickadees, sparrows (but best used as a decorative object)

DIMENSIONS:
12" w x 27" h x 5 ½" d

WEIGHT:
approximately 6½ lbs.

The house is made from old wood and a combination of old and new hardware.

OPPOSITE: IN RECENT YEARS, BRUCE HAS STARTED USING NEW FAUCETS AS BIRDHOUSE PERCHES SINCE HE CAN NO LONGER FIND OLD ONES. THE ROOF IS MADE IN PART FROM WINDOW BLINDS, AND THE MAIN PART OF THE HOUSE IS MADE FROM AN OLD PIECE OF WOOD THAT SOMEONE ACCIDENTALLY BROKE IN HIS WORKSHOP.

LEFT: THIS BRUCE HOUSE IS ALMOST THREE FEET TALL.

ABOVE: DAVID BRUCE'S FUNKY BIRDHOUSES.

His houses, however, lean more toward art than function, and that's how he sees them. He almost never builds houses to order— he builds what he likes, or what tells his story at that moment, and if someone likes the result, great. If not, that's okay, too. I first saw Bruce's funky birdhouses at Mariposa Gallery in Albuquerque, New Mexico. Their distinct look fit right in among the other art pieces.

Bruce's workshop is in a strip mall in a fringy neighborhood, and he hires people who are trying to stay clean and sober to work in the shop, piecing together his creations. There are usually a couple of "pickers" on the payroll, trolling alleys looking for wood and other choice building materials. Bruce himself still travels around the country selling his birdhouses.

Birdhouse Details

MOST LIKELY INHABITANTS:
sparrows

DIMENSIONS:
63" w x 86" h x 8½" d

WEIGHT: 1,389 lbs.

The birdhouse is built of wood with FRP (fiber-reinforced plastic) waterproofing. The exterior cladding is urethane-coated wood paneling.

OPPOSITE AND OVERLEAF: SEVENTY-EIGHT BIRD ENTRANCE HOLES MAKE UP ONE SIDE OF THE BIRD APARTMENT. THIS ELABORATE STRUCTURE FITS NICELY IN THE WOODS AT THE ANDO MOMOFUKU CENTER, IN KOMORO CITY, IN JAPAN'S MOUNTAINOUS NAGANO PREFECTURE.

PAGE 54: THE BACKSIDE OF THE APARTMENT ACCOMMODATES ONE PERSON WHO CAN REACH THE OPENING BY LADDER.

PAGE 55: THIS IS THE VIEW FROM INSIDE THE HUMAN END OF THE BIRD APARTMENT. ONCE INSIDE, THE VISITOR CAN LOOK THROUGH TINY PEEPHOLES IN A PARTITION INTO THE BIRD'S INDIVIDUAL UNITS.

WHAT COULD INSTANT RAMEN NOODLES POSSIBLY HAVE TO DO WITH A GIANT BIRDHOUSE?

Momofuku Ando was the Japanese inventor of instant ramen noodles. He developed them after WWII to help ease widespread hunger in Japan. Needless to say, the idea took off, and he made a fortune. Named in honor of the noodle company founder, the Ando Momofuku Center, in Japan's mountainous Nagano Prefecture, is a facility devoted to promoting access to nature. Since 2012, the forest surrounding the center has been home to the giant Bird Apartment, which was designed by the Tokyo-based design studio Nendo specifically for the Ando Momofuku Center.

The Bird Apartment brings together the idea of housing for both birds and people: Not only does it provide multiunit housing for birds, but it can also accommodate one person! On one side, the birdhouse has seventy-eight separate bird entrances, each leading to its own individual avian apartment. The other side, reached by a tall ladder, has an opening large enough for a human to climb through. Upon entering, a human visitor can look into the birds' units through tiny peepholes in a partition, spying on the birds without startling them.

The designers at Nendo want their work to convey a message to viewers. In this case, they want the Bird Apartment to give people a small "aha!" moment. They believe "these moments are what make our days so interesting, so rich." Surely this extraordinary combination of birdhouse and human observation deck will give any visitor many such moments!

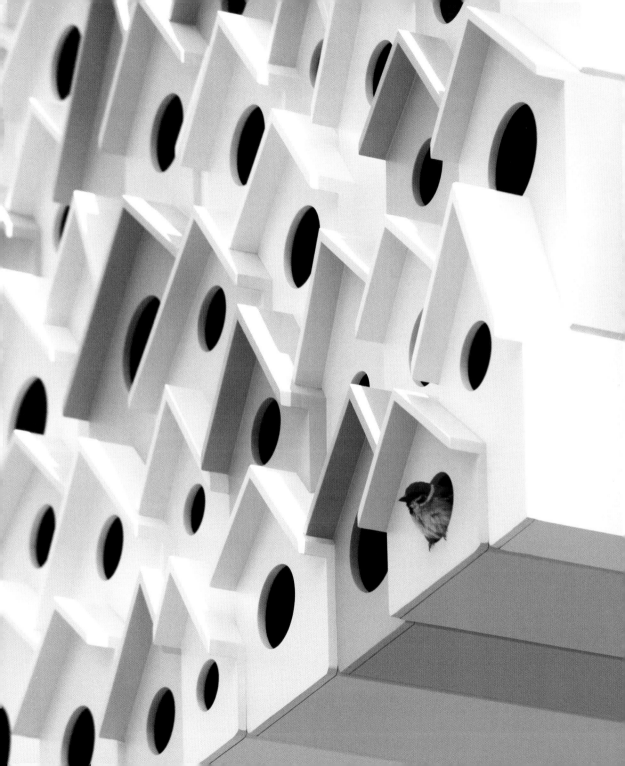

AL MOWRER'S CROOKED CREATIONS COME PURELY FROM HIS IMAGINATION. Mowrer started making his birdhouses in 2009 when his friend Chad Blecha sketched out an unusual birdhouse and asked Mowrer to build it. The process ultimately sparked Mowrer's own creative juices. Based in Denver, Colorado, he now sells his unusual and elaborate birdhouses online and at trade shows across the country.

Mowrer also builds playhouses and works in construction. He finds some of the raw materials for his birdhouses on work sites and alongside roads and railroad tracks. He has a large workshop where he stores what he finds, including piles of cedar from old fences, stacks of redwood from demolished decks, light fixtures, tree branches, bricks, lumber, and lathe strips. Plastic bins hold different items, such as pieces of glass, ropes, rusty cans, and old hinges. If there is an overall theme for the parts and pieces he chooses for his crooked creations, it's "they gotta be old."

When I asked what possessed him to make such unusual birdhouses, Mowrer told me he's inspired by everything around him and feels a constant need to be creative. "I'm one of those people who gets distracted," he says. He might be hard at work on a playhouse or some other project, and then see something in his shop from the corner of his eye and realize it would be perfect for a completely new and different project. For his playhouses, he always works from plans, but not for the birdhouses. "The birdhouses build themselves," says Mowrer. He's inspired by nature, too—a twisted tree trunk with a hole in it, a pumpkin,

Birdhouse Details

Hobbit House
DIMENSIONS:
24" w x 36" h x 30" d

WEIGHT: 40 lbs.

To mimic an old rustic look, bricks are exposed in some areas and covered with plaster-coated drywall in others.

Two-story Birdhouse (page 59)
DIMENSIONS: 32" w x 4' h

WEIGHT: 80 lbs.

The two-story birdhouse incorporates seven different types of electric lights from old lamps and chandeliers, and old metal grating for window frames was used for the stained-glass window.

OPPOSITE: MOWRER WANTED TO BUILD A BIRDHOUSE THAT RESEMBLED A HOBBIT HOME. NOTE THE MINIATURE BRICKS, WHICH ARE ACTUALLY REAL, FULL-SIZE BRICKS CUT INTO ONE-BY-HALF-INCH PIECES. MOWRER USES BOTH A BRICK SAW AND A TILE SAW TO ACHIEVE THIS LOOK. ELEVATING THE HOUSE ATOP CUT BRANCHES WAS A LAST-MINUTE IDEA; MOWRER IMAGINES A CREEK RUNNING UNDERNEATH IT.

AL MOWRER CRAFTED THIS MINIATURE STAINED GLASS WINDOW FROM METAL GRATING AND STAINED GLASS.

and even an old tree stump have jumpstarted ideas for a birdhouse.

When building a custom birdhouse, Mowrer likes to incorporate something meaningful to the customer into the final product. He built a birdhouse for his daughter using an old tree stump from her yard. The stem from a pumpkin his daughter grew made the perfect handle for the birdhouse door. Mowrer says his birdhouses are purely decorative and that generally speaking, "Birds are frightened to death of them."

SOME HAVE COM-
MENTED THAT THIS
BIRDHOUSE HAS
A TIM BURTON-
STYLE LOOK TO
IT—ODD, QUIRKY,
BUT COMPELLING.
MOWRER CALLS IT
A FANTASY DESIGN.
HE SAYS THERE WAS
NO PLAN FOR THIS
BIRDHOUSE, HE JUST
WANTED TO PLAY
WITH DIFFERENT
ROOFLINES. IT SITS
IN MOWRER'S OWN
BACKYARD ON AN
OLD VICTORIAN
POST FROM SAN
FRANCISCO.

Birdhouse Details

MOST LIKELY INHABITANTS:
wrens, chickadees, sparrows

DIMENSIONS: 16" w x 9" h x 19" d

WEIGHT: approximately 8 lbs.

- Made of birch from the Baltic peninsula, the birdhouse is ½" thick plywood, comprised of nine layers of opposing-grain ply. The roof is African mahogany and the trim is domestic alder.

- The following elements are patterned after those found in an actual Sears Craftsman kit home:

  - The fireplace.

  - Thirteen windows, two of which are located in the back of the house where the kitchen would be. One dormer window is found upstairs at the back of the house.

  - The design elements on the two doors are replicated throughout the house.

  - Rafter tails stick out around the house to support overhang.

IN THE EARLY TWENTIETH CENTURY, AMERICANS COULD MAIL ORDER A HOUSE THROUGH THE SEARS ROEBUCK CATALOG. For about $2,500, you could choose the style of home best suited for you and your family; pick out any upgrades, like maple instead of pine flooring; and order the house for delivery. Sears would bundle up the pieces, each carefully numbered, and ship the whole thing to you by rail. You or your homebuilder picked up the "kit" at the train station. This kit included everything you needed—down to the nails, floorboards, cupboards, and windows—along with a detailed set of instructions. Built-in shelving and buffets would slip right into predesigned openings, to look as though they had been crafted on-site by a cabinetmaker. The Sears Craftsman houses were very popular. Older cities all over the United States are still filled with Craftsman homes that have stood the test of time and, in fact, are highly sought after, going for prices their original owners would have found unimaginable.

The Sears Craftsman homes grew out of the American Craftsman style, which was characterized by simple, linear forms with a focus on function. It was a direct response to the ostentatious and ornate Victorian designs brought over to America from Europe. Americans yearned for a simpler style with a look that was honest and robust, not trendy. It was an aesthetic that would endure the test of time.

Jerry Shoemaker of Albuquerque, New Mexico, has been a cabinet- and furniture maker since 1997, and has always been inspired by the simplicity, function, and community focus of the Craftsman style. Shoemaker points to one of his high school shop teachers, Bob Hugill, as an instrumental figure in sparking his desire to build. He doesn't advertise and has no Web presence, but Shoemaker

CABINETMAKER JERRY SHOEMAKER PATTERNED THIS BIRDHOUSE AFTER HIS FAVORITE SEARS CRAFTSMAN HOME FROM THE 1920S. LIKE THE REAL THING, THIS BIRDHOUSE FEATURES A GENTLY SLOPING ROOFLINE, ROOMY FRONT PORCH, AND RAFTER TAILS. NOTICE THE BIRD ENTRANCE HOLE IN THE CHIMNEY.

stays busy by word of mouth. I was lucky enough to have him build my kitchen cabinets a few years ago, so when I began this project it seemed perfectly natural to have Shoemaker create a birdhouse just for this book.

When I asked him to design and build a birdhouse for this book, he decided to pattern it after one of his favorite Sears homes. Much like a Craftsman home, the birdhouse features a gently sloping roofline, a fireplace, and a front door with a three-pane design that is repeated on the windows, which have smaller panes with vertical dividers on top and large single panes on the bottom.

My Craftsman birdhome also features the front porch so loved by Craftsman homeowners. Designed to foster a sense of community with your neighbor, Craftsman front porches served as a convenient place to chat with your neighbors as they strolled past. Garages were placed in the alley out back instead of the front of the house.

In effect, I own a Sears Craftsman house suitable for birds!

THE BACKSIDE OF THE SEARS CRAFTSMAN BIRDHOUSE SHOWS OFF THE UPPER REAR DORMER WINDOW. IN A REAL
SEARS CRAFTSMAN HOME, THE HIGH WINDOWS AT THE REAR WOULD ALLOW SPACE FOR THE KITCHEN COUNTER.
THIS BIRDHOUSE VERSION FOLLOWS THE SAME DESIGN RULES.

TED FREEMAN BEGAN HIS BIRDHOUSE BUSINESS, ROUNDHOUSE WORKS, IN 2010 IN LAWRENCE, KANSAS, AFTER A LIFETIME OF WORKING IN PUBLISHING. One day Freeman saw an art deco–style birdhouse online, and despite the fact that he had no experience building anything, Freeman decided to try and build one exactly like it. Using some old cedar he had lying around, he gave it his best shot. His first attempts weren't great, but he quickly improved, and friends started to buy his birdhouses. Roundhouse Works was born.

Freeman builds birdhouses because he wants to create beautiful, artful objects using reclaimed materials. He also appreciates that birdhouses are small, receptive to detail, easy to ship, and not too time-consuming to create. As such, they are a good fit for Freeman's artistic pursuits. For Freeman, building birdhouses is like being a poet who writes sonnets—short in length but often with a powerful artistic punch. "The birds are really incidental," he says.

Hunting down the wood is one of Freeman's favorite parts of the work. Most of it comes from decrepit and abandoned barns and outbuildings, often a hundred years old or more. He finds old barn wood for sale on Craigslist, and it's not unusual for him to drive a couple hundred miles to reclaim some fine old wood. In every case, he handpicks the boards he buys. Even though he chooses each one carefully, when it comes time to build, he often ends up tossing about twenty-five percent of the boards, especially if they are weak in parts or split or contain broken nails.

Birdhouse Details

MOST LIKELY INHABITANTS: chickadees, wrens

DIMENSIONS: 12" w x 14" h x 7¾" d

WEIGHT: 4½ lbs.

ENTRANCE HOLE: 1⅛" diameter, with metal protector to discourage larger birds and predators from entering

The weatherproof roof is made of tin roofing taken from a retired chicken coop. Copper-lined holes provide ventilation, and a hatch opens for easy cleaning. The inside front of the birdhouse has a ladder so fledglings can climb out easily.

OPPOSITE: THE FLOWER-PATTERNED BIRD-HOUSE IS ONE OF FREEMAN'S POP-ULAR DESIGNS. TO CREATE THE "FLOWER," FREEMAN CHOSE ALTERNATING RED AND GRAY PIECES OF BARN WOOD. ALL OF THE WOOD USED FOR THIS HOUSE CAME FROM AN EARLY TWENTIETH-CENTURY BARN IN OLIVET, KANSAS.

Freeman uses old galvanized tin for the metalwork on his birdhouses. If the tin is rusty, the rust is usually only at the surface and hasn't yet compromised the strength of the metal. Freeman almost never uses stain or varnish on the wood; it stays as he found it. This is the style of his work, but it is also true that a brightly colored birdhouse could potentially draw the attention of predators, so a birdhouse that blends in with its environment is sometimes a safer place for birds to raise their young.

OPPOSITE: THE ENDS OF THE WOOD WEDGES CAN BE SEEN COMING TOGETHER AT THE BIRD ENTRANCE HOLE. THE METAL PROTECTOR OVER THE ENTRANCE HOLE DISCOURAGES LARGE BIRDS AND PREDATORS FROM ENTERING.

LEFT: THE BACK DOOR OF THE FLOWER-PATTERNED BIRDHOUSE OPENS FOR EASY CLEAN-OUT. NOTICE THE COPPER-LINED VENTILATION HOLE AT THE TOP. THE ROOF IS MADE OF OLD TIN FROM A RETIRED CHICKEN COOP.

Birdhouse Details

MOST LIKELY INHABITANTS:
wrens, chickadees

DIMENSIONS:
5½" w x 5 h x 5½" d

WEIGHT: 3 lbs.

The plastic material used to make the cube is 1" thick and is made from twenty-four recycled milk jugs; it is 100 percent recycled and recyclable. The cube is waterproof and opens for easy clean out. It is available in black, white, apple (red), chocolate, leaf (green), sky (blue), sand, gray, and sunset (orange).

IN 1997, BROTHERS GREG AND DAVE BENSON AND GREG'S PARTNER, TONY CIARDELLI, STARTED BUILDING ENORMOUS SKATEBOARD PARKS IN MINNEAPOLIS. They called their company TrueRide and used cutting edge, eco-friendly building materials called richlite and skatelite to construct their giant structures. TrueRide has built more than 450 skate parks throughout the United States, as well as a few in Europe and Asia.

When their company expanded and they needed more space, they moved to Duluth, Minnesota, where they rented an old, abandoned Cold War missile base to house their offices and factory. While the space served the basic needs of the company, they soon decided to find a building that reflected their values of sustainability and conservation. They bought an existing building and hired Minnesota architect David Salmela to redesign it. They started by cleaning up the polluted "brown field" that surrounded it, hauling away thirty truckloads of contaminated soil, and created an environmentally sensitive building with loads of natural light, ventilation, and low-impact landscaping. Not only did they want to make it a nice place for their seventy employees, they also wanted the structure to have as light a footprint as possible on the environment.

The Bensons and Ciardelli sold TrueRide in 2007, but by that time they had already begun the transition into their next venture. They called their new company Loll Designs. Building Adirondack chairs from recycled milk jugs is their bread and butter, but when the "boards" are cut from large 4-by-8-foot sheets of recycled plastic to make the chairs, a lot of scrap pieces are left behind. One of the designers, John Kiffmeyer, came up with an ingenious use for those scraps: the Cube Birdhouse.

OPPOSITE: I LOVE THE SIMPLE DESIGN OF THIS BRIGHT GREEN BIRDHOUSE AND THE FACT THAT IT IS MADE FROM RECYCLED PLASTIC MILK JUGS.

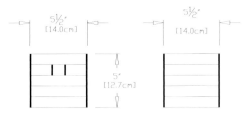

5½"
[14.0cm]

5½"
[14.0cm]

5"
[12.7cm]

product weight: 3 lbs
contains 24 reclaimed milk jugs
material thickness: ✗ 1/2˝   ✗ 5/8˝   ✗ 1˝

ABOVE: DIMENSIONS OF THE CUBE.

LEFT: LOLL DESIGNS, THE COMPANY THAT MAKES
THE CUBE BIRDHOUSE, WAS STARTED BY THE
FOUNDERS OF TRUERIDE, THE MAKERS OF GIANT
SKATEBOARD PARKS LIKE THIS ONE.

SOME OF THE MOST ELABORATE AND UNIQUE BIRD-
HOUSES I CAME ACROSS IN MY RESEARCH FOR
THIS BOOK WERE CRAFTED BY KAREL ROELOFS, A
DUTCHMAN WHO SPENT MUCH OF HIS CAREER AS
A SCULPTOR OF MARBLE IN NORTHERN ITALY. But
in 2004, when Roelofs's sculpting career was cut short by arthritis, he
decided to move back home to the Netherlands and live quietly in
the woods. Roelofs bought a small wooden house surrounded by trees
outside the Dutch village of Afferden. There, he decided to build an
elaborately decorated work shed and forty birdhouses, providing high-
end nesting spots for local birds. Roelofs found that wood was much
softer and easier on his hands than the marble he had sculpted in Italy,
so it turned out to be the perfect medium for his artistic ventures.

About a third of Roelofs's forty birdhouses are occupied each
nesting season, and all forty have been used by birds at one time or
another. He attracts six or seven different species of European cavity
nesters to his property, including swallows, for which he installs a little
ladder on the inside so their babies can climb out easily. Roelofs has
found that without the ladders, swallow fledglings have trouble exit-
ing the house and can even die as a result.

It is both unusual and delightful to find such highly decorative
birdhouses that are also extremely practical and functional. Roelofs
uses thick wood for insulation, adds proper ventilation, and makes
sure all his houses have good drainage. He builds large overhangs
above all of the entrance holes to protect baby birds from the rain,
but mostly to make it harder for birds of prey to enter. All of his

Birdhouse Details

Vogelhuisjes
(or "birdhouse" in Dutch)

MOST LIKELY INHABITANTS:
marsh tits, blue titmice, Eurasian
nuthatches, European starlings

DIMENSIONS:
6" w x 2' h x 6" d

The house is made from old
pine flooring, and some of the
wood pieces are from olive and
lime trees. Roelofs did all the
carving on the roof trim and
hand-cut the roof shingles.
The knobs are antique, and the
house opens for easy cleaning.

Fairytale (page 75)
DIMENSIONS:
6" w x 16" h x 6" d

The perch is from an old hand
grip used to spear food.

OPPOSITE: THIS CLOSE-UP OF THE
VOGELHUISJES SHOWS OFF THE BLACK
CRANE THAT ROELOFS FOUND AT A FLEA
MARKET. IT'S MADE OF EBONY AND IS
FROM THAILAND.

ROELOFS BUILT
HIS INCREDIBLE
WORKSHOP, THE
OUTSIDE OF WHICH
FEATURES LOADS
OF HIS ELABORATE
CARVINGS.

birdhouses open for easy cleaning, and they are built to the proper specifications for local birds, such as the Eurasian nuthatch, blue titmouse, and black redstart.

Roelofs finds most of his materials at local flea markets in Holland. He searches for old wood, knobs, and other antique items for as low a price as possible. Often he'll take a broken antique piece, fix it, and re-use it as something else. Most weekends Roelofs visits at least two flea markets, and he's always on the look-out for new ones in his travels.

Most people prefer Roelofs's painted birdhouses, he says, but they take longer to make. If he is using salvaged wood, he strips any varnish from its surfaces and sands every inch before adding a coat of primer. Once the birdhouse is completely assembled, Roelofs carefully paints it using acrylic paint. At the end of the process he applies two to three coats of clear varnish to protect the birdhouse from the weather. Roelofs uses varnish with an ultraviolet filter to protect the colors.

Because his workshop is so full, Roelofs builds each birdhouse outside in front of the shop. The out-side of the workshop features elaborate carvings, clay sculptures, birdhouses, and other carved-wood pieces. Any items that are not visible on workshop shelves or in open bins, Roelofs hangs on strings from the ceiling so he can see everything clearly. Having all of his flea market finds out in the open allows him to see them all at the same time, which helps to inspire the design of his next birdhouse. Any scrap of wood or decorative knob or shiny piece of metal might find its way into Roelofs's next creation.

Roelofs's sells his birdhouses at a local art market and on Etsy, but sometimes he has trouble letting go of his creations. "They are my babies," he says.

OPPOSITE: THE FAIRYTALE BIRDHOUSE TOOK ROELOFS
MORE THAN THIRTY HOURS TO BUILD. THE FRONT IS
FROM AN OLD TRADITIONAL WOODCUTTING ROELOFS
FOUND AT A FLEA MARKET. THIS TYPE OF DECORA-
TIVE WOOD PIECE WAS POPULAR IN THE PROVINCE OF
FRIESLAND IN THE NORTHERN PART OF THE NETHERLANDS
DURING THE NINETEENTH CENTURY. PART OF THE
BOTTOM OF THE BIRDHOUSE IS CAPPED BY A SHINY
YELLOW COPPER RING FROM INDIA.

TOM DUKICH BUILT HIS FIRST BIRDHOUSE IN 2000 FOR A FUND-RAISER BENEFITING THE SPOKANE ART SCHOOL. That house, inspired by the work of architect Frank Gehry, sold for $200. He built another the following year and easily sold that one, too. Encouraged by the sales, Dukich refined his design and continued to sell his stainless-steel birdhouses. Today, his houses are sold to customers all over the world. A member of one of the royal families of Europe bought one, but Tom won't reveal who it was. His creations are found in design-focused retail stores and on the Internet. Dukich likes to say that his Museum Birdhouses are "sculptures in which birds live."

To ensure that the stainless-steel houses would not get too hot for birds, Dukich did research and conducted tests to determine that the inside temperatures of a metal house are typically only a couple of degrees warmer than in a wooden house. Stainless steel doesn't hold heat like many other metals. As Dukich points out, even stainless-steel cooking pans often have some copper in the bottom to conduct heat.

Dukich is almost as interested in the creative process, which he calls "process art," as he is in the finished product. On his website, he describes the process: "Museum Birdhouses are made of high quality stainless steel, including the fasteners. All the parts are cut out with high-pressure water-jet technology to prevent heat buildup during cutting, which would discolor and warp the metal. Assembly, fitting, and finishing are all done by hand. This fabrication sequence allows the roof seams to be so precise that they are waterproof in rainy weather."

The tops of the Museum Birdhouses swing open for cleaning. More than twenty vent slots on the rear wall of the interior provide ample ventilation. There are drainage holes in the bottom, and a ladder inside helps young birds climb out as they leave the house for the first time.

Birdhouse Details

MOST LIKELY INHABITANTS:
wrens, chickadees

DIMENSIONS:
9" w x 11" h x 11" d

WEIGHT: 3½ lbs.

The Museum Birdhouse opens for easy cleaning. It is constructed of burnished stainless steel and includes a matching, corrosion-resistant pole. Since no lacquer finish coat is used, there is no chipping, flaking, or yellowing. The birdhouse is squirrel-proof (they can't chew through metal), and a variety of entrance hole sizes are available.

OPPOSITE: TOM DUKICH'S STAINLESS-STEEL BIRDHOUSES ARE INSPIRED BY THE WORK OF MODERN ARCHITECT FRANK GEHRY. PEOPLE ARE ATTRACTED TO THEIR UNUSUAL DESIGN, BUT THE BIRDS LIKE THEM, TOO.

Birdhouse Details

Trash Tree
DIMENSIONS:
33' h x 29½' w (tree);
6" w x 13" h x 6" d
(individual birdhouses)

ENTRANCE HOLES:
approximately 1½"

The Trash Tree took two weeks to construct, and is composed of old door frames, broomsticks, Dambo's neighbor's old bedroom floor, the leg from a bed, and other used wood pieces. The individual birdhouses are made from plywood that had been used as a dance floor at a music festival.

Beirut 110 Birdhouses (page 80)
MOST LIKELY INHABITANTS:
sparrows

DIMENSIONS:
7½" w x 9" h x 5" d

ENTRANCE HOLES:
approximately 2"

The birdhouses are constructed of plywood, and the windows and the birds on the front of each house were made with stencils.

THOMAS WINTHER, ALSO KNOWN AS DAMBO, WANTS TO DRAW OUR ATTENTION TO THE NATURE THAT IS DISAPPEARING FROM OUR CITIES. His birdhouses are difficult to describe, but so is Dambo, for that matter. I don't know whether to call him a street artist, designer, philosopher, or environmentalist. Maybe he is all of those things. One thing I am sure of: Winther's work is dramatic and provocative.

Dambo comments on the *absence* of nature in cities with his birdhouses. Through his various projects, he attempts to create new space for nature in the city. Dambo works to create new and useful things, like his birdhouses, out of old recycled materials. As he sees it, he's really just imitating birds, which he calls nature's "great recyclers," since they eat berries and fruit and then distribute the seeds when they pass them, thus enabling new plants to grow.

Dambo hosts workshops and events to teach others how to make their own birdhouses and how to participate in his mission. His mission statement, as stated on his website, is: "We create homes for birds and other animals that live in the city. We aim only to use trash and recycled materials. We don't charge rent. Join our flock and make your own houses."

In 2008, Dambo built 250 colorful birdhouses in two weeks and hung them in four cities throughout Denmark. This began a career in street art activism that has since sent him around the world in search of new projects. Whether you're in Beirut, Berlin, or Copenhagen, you can often spot Dambo's unique birdhouse installations hanging up around the city.

OPPOSITE: DAMBO CREATED THIS VIBRANT BLUE WALL OF BIRDHOUSES, CALLED TRASH TREE, IN COPENHAGEN, DENMARK.

Trash Tree

This vibrant blue wall of birdhouses is installed in Copenhagen, where Dambo currently lives. To create the Trash Tree, Dambo "collected old boards and planks in a local area in Osterbro, Copenhagen, and transformed them into a 33-foot-high painting/sculpture, in which all the different planks 'drew' a huge tree, and instead of leaves, the tree has seventy-five mostly green birdhouses, also made of recycled wood." The occupants of the building and the whole neighborhood are happy with the new look of the building.

Beirut 110 Birdhouses

For this project in Beirut, Dambo built 110 birdhouses during six days in 2012 as part of the Danish-Arab Urban Arts Festival. The birdhouses are in the style of classic Lebanese homes, complete with black Arabic arches. The two birds coming together on the top of each house represent the coming together of the Danish and Lebanese cultures. Dambo says he even enlisted the help of local Beirut police to install the birdhouses.

Sometimes a birdhouse isn't just a birdhouse. Dambo learned from locals in Beirut that certain colors signify allegiance to particular political parties. Some people were fearful that a birdhouse of the "wrong" color would misrepresent their political leanings. To solve that problem, Dambo grouped birdhouses of multiple colors together to neutralize any political message that might be construed. The birdhouses were hung primarily in the Hamra neighborhood, some alone and some in a grouping.

During the festival, Dambo hung a poster that read: "I made 110 birdhouses in Beirut to make people smile, and to remind them that nature is present in the big city. I designed them to look like a typical Lebanese house and have put them up on the streets of Beirut."

JUST ONE OF DAMBO'S COLORFUL BIRDHOUSES, WHICH ADORN THE STREETS OF BEIRUT, LEBANON. THE TWO BIRDS ON THE ROOF REPRESENT THE COMING TOGETHER OF TWO CULTURES, DANISH AND LEBANESE.

Birdhouse Details

DIMENSIONS: 6" w x 9¼" h

WEIGHT: approximately 2 lbs.

ENTRANCE HOLE: four sizes, ranging in diameter from just over 1" to 1½"

The plastic roof measures 7½" x 6¼" and overhangs the entrance hole by 1½"

ABOVE: THE ROOF LIFTS OFF FOR EASY CLEANING AND IS ATTACHED TO THE LADDER.

OPPOSITE: BUILT IN EUROPE OF STURDY EARTHENWARE, THIS BIRDHOUSE IS BOTH FUNCTIONAL AND DECORATIVE.

THE WORD *SLEEK* PERFECTLY DESCRIBES THE DANISH STRIPED NESTING BOX. In Europe, people call birdhouses "nesting boxes," so I'm using that phrase to describe the beautiful striped nesting box designed by Tools Design, one of Denmark's leading design firms. Their products, according to the company's designers and founders, Henrik Holbaek and Claus Jensen, range from medical equipment to household products and are characterized by a simple, innovative approach.

Holbaek and Jensen decided to make their nesting box from earthenware, rather than wood, for its durability. They also liked the look of earthenware and knew it would be easy to clean, making for a healthier birdhouse. They designed the roof to not only provide shade, but also to keep out predators like cats or squirrels. It would be almost impossible for a squirrel to hang on to the smooth, slippery front of the house, and the overhang of the roof keeps them from lying across the top to reach in and grab an egg or fledgling. The slant of the roof also keeps water from entering the nesting cavity. A ladder positioned just beneath the entrance hole is also attached to the roof piece. The entrance hole is attached to the roof and can pop out for easy cleaning and to be replaced with four different hole sizes that come with the birdhouse.

The earthenware is molded, dried, glazed, fired, and then decorated by hand. The designers chose stripes because "they are a pattern that relates to nature (like most vertical-growing vegetation)." Earthenware has excellent thermal properties and the glazed surface reflects sunlight, keeping the nesting chamber cool. And since earthenware can survive freezing temperatures, Holbaek and Jensen recommend leaving the nesting box up in the winter to provide a roosting spot for chilly birds.

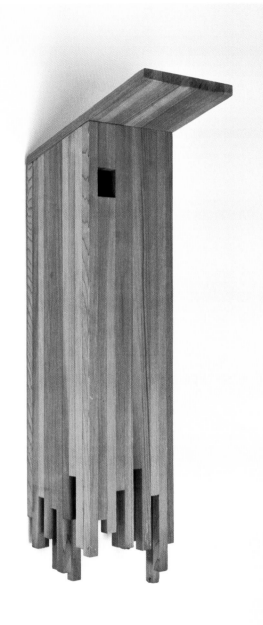

Birdhouse Details

MOST LIKELY INHABITANTS:
wrens, chickadees

DIMENSIONS:
5½" w x 22" h (at its longest point) x 5½" d

ENTRANCE HOLE:
1⅛" x 1⅛"

The roof is ten inches long and comes off for easy cleaning. Drainage and ventilation holes are drilled into the bottom of the house. To keep the house cool enough for babies, extra ventilation slots could be added to the top of the side panels.

WHEN DUFF BANGS'S MOTHER ASKED FOR A BIRDHOUSE FOR CHRISTMAS ONE YEAR, HE DIDN'T WANT TO BUY JUST ANY RUN-OF-THE-MILL BIRDHOUSE, SO HE BUILT HIS OWN.

Bangs trained as an architect and currently works for a Seattle design firm. His occasional birdhouse building is a sideline done mostly for friends and family. When he built the first birdhouse for his mother, he didn't really have a plan; it just evolved organically. He had a few unused boards from a new cedar fence, and he cut them into strips that were two feet long, a half-inch wide and a half-inch thick. Referring to the uneven "drip effect" at the bottom, Bangs says, "Although the house it not exactly symmetrical, it is balanced—it looks finished."

Because the lucky recipients of Bangs's birdhouses hang them inside on their walls as artwork, no one knows if birds would actually use them as homes. Even Bangs's mother refused to put her birdhouse outside, so recently he made her a second one for the yard. The design seems bird friendly so I imagine that, given half a chance, any lucky wren or chickadee would be happy to take up residence in one of these birdhouses.

The different-colored strips of cedar come from a variety of boards. He mixes and matches the strips to create a pleasing pattern and then adds the roof. Bangs never uses stain; he likes the way cedar "silvers" (turns gray) over time. Bangs uses wood glue and finish nails to hold the birdhouses together.

OPPOSITE: MADE FROM A VARIETY OF UNUSED CEDAR FENCING BOARDS, DUFF BANGS CRAFTED THIS MODERNISTIC BIRDHOUSE. THE OFF-CENTER ENTRANCE HOLE FITS WITH BANGS'S DESIRE TO BREAK SYMMETRY IN HIS DESIGNS. THE UNEVEN STRIPS OF CEDAR AT THE BOTTOM OF THE BIRDHOUSE FORM WHAT HE CALLS THE "DRIP EFFECT."

Birdhouse Details

Maple Leaf Flag
MOST LIKELY INHABITANTS:
wrens, sparrows

DIMENSIONS: 7' w x 7' h x 4½' d

WEIGHT: 400 lbs.

The birdhouse was lifted by a forklift onto a 9-foot post. It features seventy-five separate rooms, each with its own entrance hole.

Belgrave Inn (page 89)
MOST LIKELY INHABITANTS:
wrens, sparrows

DIMENSIONS: 5' w x 6' h x 5' d

WEIGHT: approximately 350 lbs.

Made of hundred-year-old reclaimed barn wood, the birdhouse has seventy individual rooms.

OPPOSITE: IT TOOK JOHN LOOSER TWO AND A HALF YEARS, ON AND OFF, TO BUILD THIS SEVEN-FOOT-LONG, FOUR-HUNDRED-POUND BIRDHOUSE.

EVER SINCE HE WAS FOUR OR FIVE YEARS OLD, JOHN LOOSER HAS LIKED THE IDEA OF A HOUSE UP IN THE AIR. Perhaps it's because his father made him watch *Robinson Crusoe* many times as a child. As an adult, Looser had a long career of home building "for people," but was injured in 2005. Suffering from chronic pain caused by the injury, but looking for something to keep himself busy and distracted, Looser began to build the birdhouses he had seen in his imagination since childhood. He started by making a 16-by-16-inch log birdhouse with only a few rooms. When he mounted it on a pole by the road near his house, folks took notice. Encouraged by his friends and neighbors, Looser started building bigger and bigger birdhouses. He thought, "Why not make something extreme?" Thus the name of his business, Extreme Birdhouses.

Since 2005, Looser has built more than three hundred birdhouses of all sizes, some enormous enough to have nearly one hundred separate rooms. He now has around twenty-five of his birdhouses mounted high on posts in his front yard near the busy road he lives on. Welcome signs greet visitors to his property and, in recent years, busloads of tourists and school children have begun to come for a look at his one-of-a-kind creations. The city of Belgrave has even designated Looser's property an official tourist destination. Visitors are also treated to the constant singing and chatter of the hundreds of birds living in the birdhouses.

Looser used old barn wood to make his first hundred or so birdhouses. He found that many of the old barns in his area were made of hemlock, which is a durable wood that tends to be bug

ABOVE: MOVING THE BIRDHOUSE FOR INSTALLATION TAKES A BIT OF INGENUITY. NOTE THE "POOL" (BIRD-BATH) ON THE TOP OF THE BIRDHOUSE.

OPPOSITE: THIS BIRDHOUSE SITS ON JOHN LOOSER'S PROPERTY. NOTE THE DARK PATINA OF THE HUNDRED-YEAR-OLD RECLAIMED BARN WOOD FROM WHICH IT WAS BUILT.

resistant, a good quality for both birdhouses and barns. He still uses as much old barn wood as he can find but supplements with cedar, which is also bug resistant.

Some of Looser's birdhouses weigh up to five hundred pounds and take more than two years to build. Looser often begins a large project, tires of it after a while, puts it aside, and comes back to it later when inspiration strikes.

When starting a new birdhouse, Looser lays out a flat piece of wood as the floor, on which he begins to draw out a plan. On top of the wood floor, he builds the shell of the house. He uses a few simple screws to affix the house to its wood floor. He then turns to constructing the inside rooms. Looser uses no nails on the inside construction but rather notches the inside walls of all of the rooms to fit together. This way, when it comes time

to clean the birdhouse, the walls can be easily lifted out and the inside of the birdhouse can be cleaned. For the very large birdhouses, a forklift or tractor is required to lift the house for cleaning. Looser has gone through at least four table saws over the years and burns up a saw blade every six months or so. Each little log he makes for his birdhouses has a minimum of five cuts.

Looser uses metal barn roofing material for the tops of all of his birdhouses. He even adds a little pool at the top of his large birdhouses to serve as a bird-bath. This design feature started out as an accident, when Looser made the flat part of the roof of one birdhouse a bit concave. After a rain, Looser noticed birds splashing around in the water that had collected on top of the house, so he has kept that design feature on every birdhouse since.

THE PAGODA BIRDHOUSE IS DESIGNED AND SOLD BY THE FOLKS AT MACKENZIE-CHILDS IN AURORA, NEW YORK. Known for their whimsical handmade furniture and ceramics, MacKenzie-Childs added birdhouses to their line relatively recently, but the bold designs found in the Pagoda birdhouse are typical of their style. When I first saw the Pagoda birdhouse, I was struck by its bright, strong colors and unique design. I love the mishmash of squares and stripes and dots of clashing colors.

Their corporate headquarters are located on an old dairy farm on one of the Finger Lakes, in western New York. They utilize all of the old farm buildings for office space, and the beautiful surroundings certainly influence their creations. The view from every window is breathtaking and inspiring.

Chinese pagodas, a traditional aspect of Chinese architecture, have been around for more than a thousand years and are used for religious purposes. The design of the Pagoda birdhouse takes inspiration directly from the traditional Chinese pagoda—but with a twist. Rebecca Proctor, creative director at MacKenzie-Childs, describes them as having "layers of fun and architectural detail . . . but with function."

Artisans in Asia create each Pagoda birdhouse individually. Crafted of tin and resin, each birdhouse is spot-welded together for superior strength. The roofline is designed so that water runs off the birdhouse, keeping baby birds dry. It takes five hours to hand-paint and decorate every house. No two are identical.

Birds will live in Pagoda birdhouses, but they are intended to be decorative pieces. Proctor suggests bringing the birdhouse inside during the winter to extend its life.

Birdhouse Details

DIMENSIONS:
11" w x 2' h x 11" d

WEIGHT: approximately 35 lbs.

ENTRANCE HOLE:
approximately 3"

The Pagoda birdhouse is handmade with tin and resin.

OPPOSITE: MACKENZIE-CHILDS MAKES THREE WHIMSICAL STYLES OF BIRDHOUSES. THE PAGODA BIRDHOUSE, IN THE MIDDLE, IS TWO FEET TALL AND WEIGHS ALMOST THIRTY-FIVE POUNDS.

Birdhouse Details

Red Fairy
MOST LIKELY INHABITANTS:
wrens, chickadees, sparrows

DIMENSIONS:
32" h x 8" diameter

WEIGHT: 7 lbs.

The body of the birdhouse is made from a log of red heart cedar. The roof is metal sheeting painted black with layers of red paint on top to create an aged look. The birdhouse can be opened for cleaning.

Gable (page 94)
MOST LIKELY INHABITANTS:
wrens, chickadees

DIMENSIONS:
8" w x 34" h x 8" d

WEIGHT: approximately 15 lbs.

ENTRANCE HOLE: 1⅛"

The body of this birdhouse is made from a red heart cedar log. The shingles are handmade from sheets of copper; Hopps calls them dragon-scale shingles.

ONE DAY IN 1994, JOSEPH HOPPS'S NEPHEW BROUGHT OVER SOME OLD WOOD TO BURN IN THE WOODSTOVE IN HOPPS'S WORKSHOP. "One piece was hollow and looked like a bird might like it," he says, so he saved it from the fire. There was a birdhouse competition coming up in Norman, Oklahoma, where Hopps lived at the time, so he fashioned the log into a birdhouse. He won the competition.

What began as "just toying around, just a hobby" has now become a thriving enterprise. Hopps calls his creations Arbor Castle Birdhouses, and he builds two to three hundred birdhouses each year. The more expensive birdhouses are usually much larger; some are even made as a kind of porch sculpture. He sells his birdhouses in wild bird supply stores and at art shows around the country.

Hopps likes to think of his birdhouses as woodland fairy houses. They "embody the idea of whimsy," says Hopps. He imagines that "if you were walking in the forest and came upon a magical village, these would be the types of houses you'd find there—the type of house that you'd want to live in."

Hopps is skilled enough to create every piece of his vision for his birdhouses. He crafts each component himself, except the bells above the doors. To make the vines spiraling up, Hopps cuts tiny leaves from sheets of copper and welds them onto copper wire. He uses sheets of copper to cut and form the roof shingles on some of his houses. Even the tiny door hinges are cut and formed by hand.

OPPOSITE: THE BODY OF THE RED FAIRY HOUSE IS MADE FROM A LOG OF RED HEART CEDAR. THE DOORS ARE MADE FROM CEDAR, AND THE TINY HINGES AND PULLS ARE CRAFTED FROM COPPER SHEETING. THE WHITE LADDER CLIMBING UP THE FRONT OF THE BIRDHOUSE IS MADE FROM RABBIT FENCING.

THE ROOF OF THIS
GABLED BIRDHOUSE IS
MADE FROM SHEETS OF
COPPER, AND EACH
SHINGLE IS HAND-CUT AND
FORMED. JOSEPH HOPPS
CALLS THESE "DRAGON-
SCALE" SHINGLES.

JOSEPH HOPPS AT WORK WELDING ONE OF HIS BIRDHOUSE CREATIONS.

If some material or item isn't available, he just makes it himself. Hopps explained that it takes more hours than he cares to admit to build each house. "I figure each birdhouse has taken since 1994 to build."

Hopps moved to Edom, Texas, in part because "that part of East Texas has more trees than Oklahoma," especially the red heart cedar trees that Hopps prefers. He claims that birdhouses made from this type of cedar stand up particularly well to the elements. Unfortunately, an extreme drought in Texas in 2010 and 2011 killed many of these cedars, but that made

plenty of raw material available to Hopps. Additionally, a nearby wood pulp mill sometimes has castoffs perfect for Arbor Castle Birdhouses. Edom is an artist community and has been a good fit for Hopps. He estimates that about half of the people who buy his birdhouses put them out for the birds and the other half keep them inside as art. Hopps builds them so that they are durable enough to withstand outdoor use, and he also coats the whole birdhouse with a sealer as further protection against the weather.

Birdhouse Details

MOST LIKELY INHABITANTS: wrens, chickadees

DIMENSIONS: 21" h x 7" diameter; approximately 9½' from tip of the finial to end of the ground spike

WEIGHT: 11 lbs.

ENTRANCE HOLE: 1⅓"

A stainless-steel ground spike attaches to the wooden pole for easy installation. The birdhouse also features a drainage hole.

THE WELL-KNOWN GERMAN ARCHITECT HADI TEHERANI USUALLY FOCUSES ON HIGH-RISES, OFFICE BUILDINGS, TRAIN STATIONS, AND OTHER GRAND PROJECTS. The Baya Birdhouse (manufactured and sold by the German firm GARPA) is his smallest housing project to date.

Teherani's birdhouse is inspired by the intricate nests of the Baya weaverbird found in South and Southeast Asia. Weaver-birds build their spherical nests using fine leaf fibers, grasses, and twigs, and they lash them to the limbs of trees with strands of plant material. The result is an expertly woven, extremely sturdy, spherical nest hung securely from a tree limb. The male weaver-bird builds the nest alone and then waits for a passing female to be impressed enough with his construction skills to move in and set up house.

The Baya Birdhouse consists of two teak hemispheres; the top hemisphere has a long finial, which mimics the weaverbird-built hanger. A very long bottom pole secures the house into the ground. Inside, hidden from view, is a simple system of stainless-steel rods, sleeves, and threaded joints to hold it all together. These connectors don't obstruct the bird nesting chamber, but do enable the house to be taken apart easily for cleaning. The stainless-steel parts and the high quality teak will withstand harsh weather and the test of time. Teherani describes his Baya nesting house as "organic in shape and functionality—meant for nature, inspired by nature."

OPPOSITE: ONCE INSTALLED, THE BAYA BIRDHOUSE STANDS ALMOST EIGHT FEET TALL, WITH THE BIRD ENTRANCE HOLE ABOUT FIVE FEET FROM THE GROUND. MADE OF TEAK WOOD, THIS BIRDHOUSE CONSISTS OF TWO HEMISPHERES THAT FIT TOGETHER. THEY JOIN JUST BENEATH THE STAINLESS-STEEL BIRD ENTRANCE HOLE.

Birdhouse Details

MOST LIKELY INHABITANTS:
wrens, chickadees (but is best
kept indoors as a decorative
piece)

DIMENSIONS:
The body of the house is
7½" w x 8" h x 6½" d
(16" h including roof)

WEIGHT: 6 lbs.

ENTRANCE HOLE: 1½"

The entrance hole is lined with
copper to prevent squirrels from
chewing it. The body and roof
are made from sassafras wood.

AFTER SERVING IN THE SECOND WORLD WAR, MITCH ERCEG BUILT HIS OWN HOME, BY HAND, IN EDISON, NEW JERSEY. Erceg and his wife brought up three daughters in that home, and the couple still lives there today. He has spent his working life as a carpenter, building bridges, tunnels, and houses.

Now, at age ninety, Erceg shows few signs of slowing down. About twenty years ago, he began building birdhouses—so many, in fact, that he's affectionately known as the Birdhouse King in local circles. Building birdhouses has been a fitting retirement pursuit, since Erceg has been interested in nature—and birds in particular— since he was a kid. Erceg's parents, originally from Croatia, always kept a parakeet that reportedly spoke with a Croatian accent, just like its owners.

In each birdhouse, Erceg layers different varieties of wood and bleaches the surfaces of some pieces to highlight the contrast between them. His carpentry skills are obvious in the fine detailing of

OPPOSITE: MITCH ERCEG CRAFTED THIS BIRDHOUSE FROM THE LOG OF A SASSAFRAS TREE. HE USED A WOOD-BURNING TOOL TO ETCH THE FLOWERS ON THE FRONT AND LEGS. THE SCALLOPED EDGE ALONG THE ROOFLINE WAS MADE BY CUTTING SLICES OF AN ENGLISH YEW. THE PINECONE-LIKE OBJECT AT THE TOP OF THE HOUSE IS A THIKA POD FROM KENYA. ERCEG HALVES THE PODS AND ATTACHES THEM FLUSH TO MANY OF HIS BIRDHOUSES. THE FRONT FACE OF THE BIRDHOUSE IS BOX ELDER (FROM THE PIECE THAT HIS DAUGHTER GAVE TO HIM). THE RED IN THE WOOD IS A RESULT OF EXCREMENT FROM BUGS THAT ONCE INHABITED THE TREE. ERCEG BLEACHED THE FRONT TO BRING OUT THE CONTRAST BETWEEN THE RED STREAKING AND THE LIGHTER WOOD.

NOTE THE LEVEL OF DETAIL, INCLUDING THE BUTTERFLY ERCEG PLACES ON EACH OF HIS BIRDHOUSES IN HONOR OF HIS MOTHER.

each house. In honor of his mother, who loved butterflies, Erceg adds a small butterfly to each house. He keeps himself busy painstakingly crafting two new birdhouses each week.

Finding wood is never a problem. Mitch is so well known that neighbors and even local UPS and FedEx drivers bring him interesting-looking wood they find on their routes. He has a real passion for wood. His daughter Jacquee gave him a piece of beautiful box elder as a Christmas present one year. He was so ex-cited and preoccupied with thinking up ways to use it in a birdhouse that he had trouble sleeping that night.

Erceg sells most of his birdhouses at arts-and-crafts shows and through his website. Jacquee helps him at shows and created and maintains his website. Buyers come from as far away as Europe, and a few collectors own several dozen of Erceg's works. Even former President George H. W. Bush owns one of Erceg's birdhouses!

NOTE THE TINY ETCHING OF A FLOWER AND THE COPPER LINING INSIDE THE BIRD ENTRANCE HOLE.

23 | J SCHATZ BIRDHOUSES
Greene, New York

"YOU CAN'T LIVE WHERE I DO AND NOT APPRECIATE THE BIRDS," SAYS JIM SCHATZ, PRESIDENT AND DESIGNER OF J SCHATZ CERAMIC PRODUCTS. Schatz has been making art since his college days in the 1990s. After college, he worked in advertising and Web design in New York to support himself, while working on his art in his spare time. When his long-time partner died in 2004, Schatz moved his design studio from the East Village in New York City to the woods in upstate Greene, New York, where he now lives with his current partner and works as a full-time artist. Together, they have transformed his creek-side home into an indoor/outdoor living space with a beautiful garden filled with J Schatz bird products.

His move from the city has been transformative. Living along-side the beautiful Genegantslet Creek inspired him to create a number of birding products. In 2012, he created his Nut Birdhouse, a simple, well-designed, bird-friendly house. It is both gorgeous and highly functional, a combination of characteristics rarely found in the same birdhouse. Schatz incorporates all of his products into his daily life and "wonder-certifies" everything he makes: For each bird-house, he produces a prototype or mockup of the idea and lives with it for a while. If it continues to inspire wonder in him throughout the weeks, months, and years that he lives with it, he will put it into production.

Birdhouse Details

Nut House
MOST LIKELY INHABITANTS:
bluebirds, nuthatches, chickadees, titmice

DIMENSIONS:
9⅜" h x 5 ⅛" diameter

WEIGHT: 3½ lbs.

ENTRY HOLE: 1½" diameter

ALUMINUM COVER:
1⅞" h x 5 ⅜" diameter

ALUMINUM MOUNTING POLE:
6' x 1¼" diameter

Has a drainage hole in the bottom.

OPPOSITE: THIS EASTERN BLUEBIRD IS COMING IN FOR A LANDING ON THE NUT HOUSE.

ABOVE: THE STONEWARE EGG BIRDHOUSE IS ONE OF
J SCHATZ'S MOST POPULAR DESIGNS.

OPPOSITE: HAND-BUILT OF DURABLE STONEWARE,
THE NUT BIRDHOUSE RESEMBLES AN ACORN.

Birdhouse Details

Egg House

MOST LIKELY INHABITANTS:
wrens, chickadees

DIMENSIONS: 8" h x 6" w

WEIGHT: 1 lb.

ENTRY HOLE: 1⅛" diameter

VINYL-COATED HANGING WIRE:
2'

The Egg Birdhouse is made of ceramic stoneware. An aluminum perch is sealed with a clear nylon hole protector. The aluminum bottom has ventilation and drainage holes as well as a clean-out hole. The aluminum bottom, perch, and vinyl-coated hanging wire are all rust resistant.

NUT BIRDHOUSE

Each house is handmade in Schatz's studio, one at a time. Schatz built his Nut Birdhouse to specifications that attract bluebirds, chickadees, nuthatches, and titmice. It has a snug but removable aluminum cover that not only is easy to monitor for unwanted visitors like house sparrows and starlings, but is also easy to clean out when nesting birds have moved on. The body of the Nut house is cast in very durable stoneware and is built to withstand year-round temperature extremes. Before it's fired, Schatz scratches the inside wall of the birdhouse, just below the entrance hole, to create a "ladder" that serves as an easy way out for baby birds. The house is fired, glazed, and then fired again. The whole process takes about two weeks.

EGG BIRDHOUSE

First crafted in 2005 and made of durable, handcrafted stoneware, the Egg Birdhouse is one of Schatz's most popular designs. This birdhouse is also functional. The perch is removable, thus making the house safer from predators during nesting season. Plus, it's tough for any predator to hang on to high-gloss, smooth stoneware. It also has a clean-out as well as ventilation holes.

DEFYING ALL ODDS, HURRICANE KATRINA SPURRED ARTISTIC EXPRESSION OF EVERY KIND—EVEN BIRD-HOUSES. When New Orleans resident and artist Ryan Ballard and his family lost their home in the hurricane, they were displaced to Colorado Springs, Colorado, for a couple of years. During their time in Colorado, Ballard decided to make birdhouses with debris left over from Katrina. To prepare for the project, Ballard drove home to New Orleans to pick up pieces of broken homes, including his own. In 2005, he built birdhouses for a dozen friends and relatives as Christmas presents.

When the American Democracy Project, a sponsor of thought-provoking art projects and exhibitions that address political and social issues, heard about Ballard's birdhouses made from the mess of Katrina, the group invited him to participate in the exhibition *Raise Your Voice!* at the University of Missouri. Ballard's "piece" was a series of ten birdhouses called "Forced Migration." After that, Ballard's Katrina birdhouses were in high demand and spent about a year and a half traveling from one art show to another all around the country.

Ryan Ballard is back living in New Orleans once again. To him, New Orleans culture "embraces glorious dichotomies, both wonderful and brazen. There is a reverence for pirates and anyone who can suspend social norms. We show that every year at Mardi Gras." Pirate imagery is not uncommon in Ballard's birdhouses.

When Ballard returned to New Orleans, he continued to build birdhouses, which came to the notice of city officials, who

Birdhouse Details

Creole House
MOST LIKELY INHABITANTS:
wrens, chickadees, sparrows

DIMENSIONS:
2' w x 1½' h x 2' d

WEIGHT: approximately 15 lbs.

Has a hatch for easy cleaning.

Pitot House (page 108)
MOST LIKELY INHABITANTS:
wrens, chickadees, sparrows

DIMENSIONS: 3' w x 2' d x 2' h

WEIGHT: approximately 15 lbs.

OPPOSITE: NOTICE THE MINIATURE TRUMPET AND SKELETON IMAGE ON THE ENTRANCE-HOLE SIDE OF THE CREOLE BIRDHOUSE. THIS HOUSE IS TWO FEET WIDE BY TWO FEET DEEP.

PATTERNED AFTER THE HISTORIC TWO-HUNDRED-YEAR-OLD PITOT HOUSE IN NEW ORLEANS, THIS BIRDHOUSE
MEASURES THREE FEET WIDE AND WEIGHS FIFTEEN POUNDS.

THIS CLOSE-UP REVEALS MORE MARDI GRAS BEADS AND TRINKETS AND SOME OF BALLARD'S DETAILED DRAWINGS AND COLLAGE.

commissioned Ballard to build birdhouses that represented the iconic architecture and neighborhoods of the city. He titled the series *No Place Like NOLA* (New Orleans, Louisiana). The yellow Creole House from that series represents the French Quarter, Vieux Carre. This group of fourteen houses was displayed for three years at the New Orleans Botanical Gardens. "Birds lived in them the whole time," says Ballard.

The Creole House, along with others from the series, features a mix of old and new elements, such as new Mardi Gras beads with old scraps of wood and salvaged furniture. The Pitot House is based on the more than two-hundred-year-old Pitot House on Bayou St. John, the only Creole colonial country house in New Orleans that is open to the public. James Pitot

was an early mayor of New Orleans and lived in the home from 1810 to 1819. Ballard patterned another birdhouse after the New Orleans home of artist Edgar Degas. One birdhouse he built for the series that didn't make the final cut was based on a FEMA trailer.

Although a Ballard birdhouse is somewhat functional, most people keep theirs inside as decorative objects. Each birdhouse is made from salvaged lumber and scrap and is covered with Ballard's artwork. Trinkets, beads, and other Mardi Gras throws are featured on both the Creole and the Pitot birdhouses. "My most successful work violates the boundaries between kitsch, craft, and 'fine' art, and is full of symbolic ritual and psychological imagery," explains Ballard.

SOME YEARS AGO, NATHAN WIELER, THE FOUNDER OF A COMPANY CALLED MODERN BIRDHOUSES, BOUGHT A BIRDHOUSE AT A SILENT AUCTION FOR CHARITY. He loved the house and struck up a conversation with its maker, North Carolina architect Dail Dixon. Dixon and Wieler discovered that they shared a passion for both birdhouses and modern design, so together they hatched a plan to form a company that would build and sell birdhouses.

Designing birdhouses is nothing new for Dixon. His father, Fred, won the Bird Box Prize at the 1925 North Carolina State Fair for a birdhouse he built resembling a log cabin, and Dail has been designing and building birdhouses in his spare time since he was a child.

Dixon designed a series of birdhouses, including the Ralph, that were inspired by the home designs of three architects (J. R. Davidson, Richard Neutra, and Ralph Rapson) who participated in the groundbreaking Case Study Houses program, which was implemented in the mid-1940s.

The birdhouse shown here honors Ralph Rapson, one of the great pioneers of twentieth-century modern home design in America. It was inspired by Rapson's iconic 1945 Greenbelt House, which features an enclosed garden and angled rooflines. Rapson's Greenbelt House was among the earliest in the Case Study Houses program, which was hugely influential in the development of modern residential design.

The first Ralph birdhouse was produced in 2004. I own one and love it—it's a beautiful birdhouse, with simple, clean lines. Each one is built by hand using fine materials, such as sustainably

Birdhouse Details

MOST LIKELY INHABITANTS: chickadees, titmice, wrens

DIMENSIONS: 6"w x 6"d x 6" h (body), 10" w x 9" d (roof)

ENTRANCE HOLE: 1⅜" diameter

The birdhouse is constructed of sustainably harvested wood. The roof is made from sandblasted ¼" thick aluminum plate, aluminum dowels, and stainless-steel fasteners, which prevent rust and corrosion. The well-ventilated structure has a bottom that opens for easy cleaning.

OPPOSITE: INSPIRED BY THE WORK OF ARCHITECT RALPH RAPSON, THIS MODERN BIRDHOUSE IS NOT ONLY SOUGHT AFTER BY HUMANS BUT IS BUILT WITH BIRDS IN MIND.

ARCHITECT DAIL DIXON DESIGNED THIS SERIES OF THREE MODERN BIRDHOUSES. EACH IS HAND-BUILT FROM SUSTAINABLY HARVESTED WOOD. CHECK OUT THE AMPLE VENTILATION JUST UNDER THE ROOF OF EACH HOUSE.

harvested teak and sandblasted aluminum plate. It takes craftsmen about four hours to build each birdhouse. A master carpenter cuts and sands the wood by hand and then applies natural linseed oil, which protects the wood from rain, mildew, and UV rays.

Elegant design isn't Wieler and Dixon's only priority. Their Modern Birdhouses are also built for the birds: Initial designs included a perch that the makers later removed after learning that a perch allows predators to easily enter the birdhouse.

A CLOSE-UP OF THE MODERNISTIC ROOFTOP.

Birdhouse Details

Barn Wood

MOST LIKELY INHABITANTS:
wrens, chickadees

DIMENSIONS:
14" w x 36" h x 12" d

WEIGHT: 25 lbs.

Holmquist crafted the birdhouse from very old barn wood, drawer pulls, and hinges. An antique lock and antique decorative grating were used on the front.

WHEN ROLF HOLMQUIST MOVED TO THE BLUE RIDGE MOUNTAINS IN NORTH CAROLINA IN 1994, HE KNEW HE WANTED TO MORE FULLY DEVELOP HIS ARTISTIC TALENTS IN THE AREA OF CRAFT, PARTICULARLY IN WOODWORKING. He had long been a painter, but he figured that if he was going to be living among some of the finest crafts-people in the country, he might as well reinvent himself. That's when he started building birdhouses.

Born in Sweden, Holmquist has been in America since he was fourteen years old but still carries a trace of an accent. His birdhouses also have a distinctive Scandinavian flavor to them. Holmquist uses antique and used items for his creations, as well as wood reclaimed from old barns. His home, a log cabin he built himself an hour north of Asheville, is near the local recycling center and landfill. Friends passing on their way to the dump will stop at Holmquist's house first to see if any of their rejects might be perfect for future birdhouse projects. Even the workers at the landfill call Holmquist if they notice something that they think he might use—old chairs and beat-up metal grating, for instance. By his own assessment, one of the sheds on his property looks like something out of the show *Hoarders*.

Although he's made more than four hundred birdhouses during the almost twenty years he has practiced the craft, no two are alike. Most of his birdhouses are sold through the New Morning Gallery in Asheville, North Carolina, but he sells in other shops and galleries around the country as well.

OPPOSITE: A SMALL BRIAR WOOD STUDIO PLAQUE ADORNS THE FRONT OF THE BARN WOOD BIRDHOUSE. LOOK CLOSELY FOR THE OLD LOCK AND THE PIECE OF OLD PIPE.

RIGHT: THE NAME OF THIS BIRDHOUSE,
AMBER WAVES OF GRAIN, IS TAKEN
FROM A FRAGMENT OF A LICENSE PLATE
HANGING NEAR THE BOTTOM. PARTS
OF A CRIB EXTEND OUT ON BOTH SIDES
BENEATH THE ROOF, WHICH IS MADE OF
TIN TAKEN FROM AN OLD CHURCH IN
TRYON, NORTH CAROLINA. THE METAL
PIECE ON THE FRONT IS FROM A DOOR
KNOCKER, AND VINTAGE DRAWER PULLS
CAN BE FOUND HERE AND THERE. THE
BIRDHOUSE MEASURES 3½ FEET HIGH
AND WEIGHS IN AT 40 POUNDS.

OPPOSITE: OVER-THE-TOP BIRDHOUSE
IS OVER FIVE FEET IN LENGTH, NOT
INCLUDING THE MOUNTING POST.
MADE FROM MANY DIFFERENT
SALVAGED MATERIALS, ITS MOST
NOTABLE FEATURE IS THE BIRD
OVERHANGING THE TOP.

Birdhouse Details

Over-the-Top

MOST LIKELY INHABITANTS:
wrens, chickadees

DIMENSIONS:
24" w x 5' h x 14" d

WEIGHT: 30 lbs.

ENTRANCE HOLE: 1¼" diameter

The base and body of the birdhouse are made from old barn wood, and the structure can be opened for easy cleaning. A bird cast in resin is perched out front atop antique lamp parts, and antique chairs form two spiral lengths on the front of the house.

Birdhouse Details

DIMENSIONS:
11" w x 15" h x 11" d

WEIGHT: 8 lbs.

Items used to craft the birdhouse include dried blueberries, cranberries, papaya, and cherries; almonds; birdseed including millet, milo, black-oil sunflower, safflower, and flax; juniper greens and berries; and tallow berries (the white berries along the roofline under the cardinal).

BIRCH AND VELMA SMITH STARTED BUILDING BIRDSEED BLOCKS AND CYLINDERS IN THEIR KITCHEN IN 1996. They are now one of the largest manufacturers of birdseed blocks and birdseed gifts in the nation. In 2000, they began making small birdseed houses to sell at Christmastime, and since then have sold more than one hundred thousand. Their company is Mr. Bird, and they have made many thousands of customers and millions of birds happy with their birdseed offerings.

I asked Birch Smith (Mr. Bird) to build a one-of-a-kind birdhouse for this book. He made a few sketches for a house much larger than they usually make and gave them to Greg Williams, who builds many of the wooden shells for the Smiths' birdseed houses. It took Williams about four hours to build the wooden shell for this one, but it took Smith's wife, Velma (Mrs. Bird), two days to decorate it. Hot glue gun in hand, Velma pulled out all the stops.

Birds won't nest in this house, but they love to eat it. the Smiths used different types of seeds and berries to adorn the shell, most of which are edible. The seed is stuck to the wooden surface of the birdhouse with edible gelatin, which is perfectly safe and tasty for birds. The berries, greenery, and other larger decorative items are held in place with glue.

When asked if building a large custom birdhouse for the book inspired him to build more, Smith just laughed. The time and effort it took to build this birdhouse will guarantee that it remains one of a kind!

OPPOSITE: THIS ONE-OF-A-KIND BIRDSEED BIRDHOUSE WON'T INSPIRE BIRDS TO NEST, BUT IT WILL PROVIDE DINNER. FIVE DIFFERENT TYPES OF DRIED FRUIT, INCLUDING PAPAYA, ARE AMONG THE DOZENS OF DECORATIVE ITEMS ON THIS BIRDHOUSE.

RIGHT: A CLOSE-UP OF THE BIRDHOUSE
ON PAGE 119 SHOWS THE LEVEL OF
DETAIL. LOOK CLOSELY TO SEE THE
ALMONDS ON THE BOTTOM RIGHT.

OPPOSITE: THIS SMALLER BIRDSEED
BIRDHOUSE IS AMONG THE PRODUCTS
SOLD BY BIRCH SMITH (MR. BIRD). IT
SPARKED THE IDEA TO HAVE MR. BIRD
BUILD AN OVER-THE-TOP VERSION
FOR ME.

OF ALL THE BIRDHOUSES IN THIS BOOK, THIS ONE HAS, PERHAPS, HAD THE MOST IMPACT ON NATURE HERSELF.

Purple martins love to eat flying insects. According to the Nature Society, purple martins are capable of consuming up to two thousand mosquitoes per day, which helps explain why people love to have them living nearby. These dark purple colony nesters used to build their homes in tree cavities before development and urban sprawl eliminated most of their natural nesting sites. Farmers also drained many of the swamps and wetlands where martins fly to find insects. As a result, the purple martin population began to decline. But there is hope: While human activity has severely impacted the purple martin population, we have also been important in their resurgence.

According to the Cornell Lab of Ornithology website, the purple martin is the largest member of the swallow family in North America. They're found mostly east of the Rockies, where they have been almost entirely dependent upon manmade housing for more than one hundred years. The few martins found west of the Rockies still tend to use tree cavities as nesting sites. They migrate to South America for the winter, but just before they head south, in the late summer, they join together in enormous premigratory flocks of up to one hundred thousand birds. These massive flocks are stunning to behold.

In the early 1960s, J. L. Wade's television antenna manufacturing business in Griggsville, Illinois, was beginning to wane. But Wade was an entrepreneur, and he knew Griggsville had too many

Birdhouse Details

MOST LIKELY INHABITANTS: purple martins; if not monitored properly, can be taken over by sparrows or European starlings

DIMENSIONS: 18" w x 12" h x 12" d

WEIGHT: 10 lbs.

ENTRANCE HOLES: 2⅛"

The birdhouse has twelve martin nesting compartments, each measuring 6" square. Dry-nest subfloors lift the floor of each compartment away from moisture. Guardrails were added to keep baby birds from falling out of the nest prematurely. Additionally, the birdhouse features a roof perch, swing-out doors for easy cleaning, winter doorstops, and all-aluminum construction.

OPPOSITE: A MALE PURPLE MARTIN IN FLIGHT WITH AN INSECT OR TWO GRIPPED FIRMLY IN HIS BEAK.

mosquitoes. Wade remembered his father keeping wooden martin houses along the banks of their riverside home and knew that those martins kept the mosquito population around the yard under control. He figured that if he could find a creative way to help Griggsville's citizens keep mosquitoes at bay, he might, at the same time, create a new business. Joining forces with bird expert T. E. Musselman, Wade began building purple martin houses, which he called the M12K Pioneer. (The M stands for Musselman, the number 12 represents the number of bird compartments in the house, and K stands for kit, since it came in a kit form.) Little did he know that his innovations would be instrumental in bringing the beloved purple martin back from the brink of extinction.

Wade began building large, lightweight houses for the martins. Martins nest in colonies and prefer a house with many nesting holes, and martin houses should be cleaned out after use and closed off in the winter so that house sparrows and other unwanted guests can't take over. The trouble with old wooden apartment-style birdhouses is that they are heavy and thus difficult to clean out and close up. Wade's design solved these problems and the martins took to the houses instantly. Aluminum, which Wade had used to make TV antennas, turned out to be the perfect material for martin houses. The aluminum was lightweight and reflected the heat so babies kept cool.

Wade installed forty of his new martin houses along the streets of Griggsville in 1962. They were replaced in 1992 for aesthetic reasons—the originals had faded a bit. The new forty houses are still going strong. Many imitations have come and gone since Wade built his first M12K Pioneer martin house, but none have come close to matching its quality and design. Wade lived a long life, long enough to witness a nationwide resurgence of the purple martin population.

THE PIONEER WAS THE FIRST ALUMINUM PURPLE MARTIN HOUSE, AND ITS INNOVATIVE DESIGN HELPED SAVE THE SPECIES FROM EXTINCTION.

WORKERS AT TRIO MANUFACTURING INSTALLING ONE OF THEIR SUPER-CASTLE MARTIN HOUSES ON THE GROUNDS OF THE FACTORY IN GRIGGSVILLE, ILLINOIS.

BIRDHOUSE
RESOURCES

NESTING CHART

More than eighty species of North American birds nest in cavities and will use birdhouses. This chart includes the most commonly found cavity nesters in North America.

House sparrows and European starlings commonly nest in birdhouses but are not included in this list because they are nonnative birds (in North America) that aggressively displace native species and should not be encouraged. House sparrows usually require an entrance hole of 1½" or larger. European starlings typically need a 1⁹/₁₆" or larger entrance hole. Often, birdhouses are built to exclude these birds.

THIS MALE EASTERN BLUEBIRD DOES NOT NEED
A PERCH TO ENTER THE NESTING CAVITY.
NO PERCH IS PREFERRED, AS PREDATORS CAN
USE IT TO MORE EASILY ENTER BIRDHOUSES.

NAME	SIZE OF FLOOR
Chickadee	4" x 4"
Titmouse	4" x 4"
Nuthatch	4" x 4"
House Wren	4" x 4"
Bewick's Wren	4" x 4"
Carolina Wren	4" x 4"
Screech Owl	8" x 8"
Wood Duck	12" x 12"
Purple Martins	6" x 6"

WOODPECKERS	
Downy	4" x 4"
Hairy	6" x 6"
Flicker	7" x 7"

BLUEBIRDS	
Eastern	4" x 4"
Western	5" x 5"
Mountain	5" x 5"

BIRDHOUSE SPECIFICATIONS FOR COMMON SPECIES

HEIGHT OF ENTRANCE ABOVE THE FLOOR	DIAMETER OF HOLE	HEIGHT ABOVE THE GROUND	PREFERRED HABITAT
4" – 7"	1 ⅛"	5' – 15'	Woods/edge
6" – 8"	1 ¼"	5' – 15'	Woods/edge
6" – 8"	1 ¼" – 1 ⅜"	5' – 20'	Woods/edge
4" – 7"	1 ⅛" – 1 ¼"	5' – 10'	Woods/yard
4" – 7"	1 ¼"	5' – 10'	Woods/yard
4" – 7"	1 ½"	5' – 10'	Woods/yard
9" – 12"	3"	10' – 30'	Woods
10" – 18"	4"w x 3"h (oblong)	6' – 30'	Woods near water
1"	2 ⅛"	10' – 20'	Open fields near water
8" – 12"	1 ¼"	5' – 15'	Woods
10" – 14"	1 ½"	8' – 20'	Woods
10" – 20"	2 ½"	6' – 30'	Woods
6" – 7"	1 ½"	5' – 6'	Fence rows and fields
6" – 7"	1 ⁹⁄₁₆"	5' – 6'	Fence rows and fields
6" – 7"	1 ⁹⁄₁₆"	5' – 6'	Fence rows and fields

Nesting chart created by John Schaust and Brian Cunningham of Wild Birds Unlimited. Used with permission of Jim Carpenter, President and CEO of Wild Birds Unlimited.

WHAT TO LOOK FOR IN A FUNCTIONAL BIRDHOUSE

SOME BIRDS DON'T KNOW WHAT'S GOOD FOR THEM AND WILL NEST IN BIRDHOUSES THAT ARE UNSUITABLE, OR EVEN DANGEROUS.
Birds sometimes nest in a birdhouse with an entrance hole that is too big, giving predators an easy way in. Others might choose to nest in a metal birdhouse without realizing that the house will get too hot in the summer for their babies to survive. When choosing a birdhouse to put outside for the birds, be careful to choose a functional birdhouse, one that is suitable for the species of bird you wish to attract and that will give your birds the best chance of survival. Most birds that use birdhouses nest alone—one family per house—but house sparrows and European starlings, found throughout the country, will nest just about anywhere, singly or in a group. The purple martin is the rare species that almost always nests in colonies, preferring large multi-chamber birdhouses.

FEATURES OF A FUNCTIONAL BIRDHOUSE
DRAINAGE
Holes in the bottom corners of the birdhouse are important to allow for adequate drainage. Holes in the middle of the bottom are usually blocked by the nest, so these will not provide enough drainage. Keeping nests and babies dry increases young birds' chance of survival. It is also helpful if the roof of the birdhouse is slanted, with an overhang, so that water can easily run off.

VENTILATION
Holes, on side panels, near the top of the house will allow heat to escape.

INSULATION
For proper insulation against the heat and cold, wood should be at least ¾" thick; recycled plastic should be at least ½" thick. Wood and recycled plastic are the best materials for birdhouse construction.

THESE BLUEBIRD HOUSES WERE DESIGNED BY WILD BIRDS UNLIMITED AND INCLUDE ALL THE FEATURES NESTING BIRDS NEED. BOTH THE WOOD AND RECYCLED PLASTIC VERSIONS (SHOWN HERE) OFFER STURDY CONSTRUCTION AND WALLS THAT ARE THICK ENOUGH TO INSULATE THE BIRDS AGAINST HEAT AND COLD.

VENTILATION

LADDER

CLEAN-OUT

DRAINAGE

HOLE SIZE (*See Chart*)

Birdhouse entrance holes must suit the bird you want to attract and, oftentimes more important, exclude the bird you do not want to attract.

BIRDHOUSE SIZE (*See Chart*)

Different birds are attracted to different-sized nesting boxes. By using a birdhouse that is the right size and design for a particular species, you give birds the best shot at raising their young successfully.

CLEAN OUT

It's important to be able to easily clean out your birdhouse. This prevents a buildup of mites and other parasites. Clean out your birdhouses after each use, in the fall, and in very early spring.

PERCHES

Birds do not need a perch to enter a natural cavity so they do not need one to enter a birdhouse. A perch will allow sparrows and other predators easy access to eggs and nestlings.

LADDER

The inside of your birdhouse should have a ladder or grooves under the entrance hole to help baby birds climb out. Except for a ladder, the inside of your nesting box should have no obstructions, perches, or ledges of any kind.

STURDY CONSTRUCTION

No one wants a birdhouse to fall apart when eggs or nestlings are present. Look for a sturdy, well-constructed birdhouse that will withstand time and the elements. Securely mount or hang your birdhouse.

PROPER CARE OF A FUNCTIONAL BIRDHOUSE

No additional paint or stain is needed for your nesting box. Light-colored woods or light-colored recycled plastic is best, as dark colors can absorb sunlight and make the birdhouse too hot.

Sometimes a birdhouse will be used several times during a nesting season. Clean out your nesting box after each use. Remove the old nest and brush out the inside of the house with a stiff brush. If the house is particularly dirty, scrub it out with soapy water, rinse it well, and allow it to fully dry.

Some birdhouse owners plug their birdhouse entrance holes in late fall and throughout the winter to prevent house sparrows or starlings from roosting there during the winter. If sparrows or starlings are numerous in your area, you might consider doing this if you want to discourage them from using that birdhouse come spring. However, birdhouses make nice winter roosting spots for chilly birds so it's really best not to plug them up.

At the end of the nesting season, make any necessary repairs to your birdhouse. Don't wait until spring. Some birds start nesting very early, well before some of us think about doing our springtime chores.

BLUEBIRDS TYPICALLY NEST EARLY IN THE SPRING, SOMETIMES WHEN SNOW IS STILL ON THE GROUND.

THIS ART INSTALLATION WAS
CREATED BY JOSEF BERNHARDT
IN VIENNA, AUSTRIA.

BIRDHOUSE MAKERS
CONTACT INFORMATION

To contact the designers whose birdhouses are featured in this book, or to purchase a birdhouse, use the contact information listed below.

THOMAS BURKE
www.TFBurkebirdhomes.com
PAGE 20

WINESTONE BIRDHOUSES
winestonebirdhouses.virb.com
PAGE 26

ANTHONY CATEAUX
www.acdesignironworks.com or
anthonycateaux@shaw.ca
PAGE 30

LORENZO PADILLA
www.lorenzoswoodworks.com or
l.lenchito@aol.com
PAGE 34

LONDON FIELDWORKS
www.londonfieldworks.com
PAGE 38

ROBERT SHUPING
www.rsswoodworks.com
PAGE 42

DAVID BRUCE
www.weatheredwonders.com or
(602) 576-7376
PAGE 46

NENDO
www.nendo.jp/en/
ANDO MOMOFUKU CENTER
momofukucenter.jp/
(in Japanese only)
PAGE 50

CROOKED CREATIONS
on Facebook or call Al Mowrer at
(303) 717-7016
PAGE 56

JERRY SHOEMAKER
(505) 515-4306
PAGE 60

TED FREEMAN
www.roundhouseworks.etsy.com
PAGE 64

LOLL DESIGNS
www.lolldesigns.com
PAGE 68

KAREL ROELOFS
http://karel-spot.blogspot.nl/.
PAGE 72

TOM DUKICH
His birdhouses can be purchased
through www.tomdukich.com
PAGE 76

**THOMAS "DAMBO"
WINTHER**
www.thomasdambo.com
PAGE 78

TOOLS DESIGN
www.toolsdesign.com. This
birdhouse can be purchased
through www.evasolo.com
PAGE 82

DUFF BANGS
Etsy at Duffrey93
PAGE 84

JOHN LOOSER
www.extremebirdhouse.com or
(519) 357-9595
PAGE 86

MACKENZIE-CHILDS
www.MacKenzie-Childs.com
PAGE 90

JOSEPH HOPPS
www.arborcastlebirdhouses.com
PAGE 92

BAYA BIRDHOUSE
The Baya Birdhouse can be
purchased at
www.garpa.com
PAGE 96

MITCH ERCEG
www.birdhouseking.com
PAGE 98

JIM SCHATZ
www.jschatz.com
PAGE 102

RYAN BALLARD
www.artgobang.com
PAGE 106

MODERN BIRDHOUSES
www.modernbirdhouses.com
PAGE 110

ROLF HOLMQUIST
rolfholmquist1@frontier.com
PAGE 114

MR. BIRD
www.mrbird.com
PAGE 118

M12K MARTIN HOUSES
M12K Martin Houses can be
purchased at
www.naturehouseinc.com.
For information about purple
martins, contact The Nature Society
at www.naturesociety.org
PAGE 122

PHOTO CREDITS

Front cover: Dave and Steve Maslowski (upper left),
London Fieldworks (upper right), J Schatz
(lower left), Amadeus Leitner (lower right)
Back cover: Thomas Dambo Winther
Endpapers: Ingólfur Bjargmundsson/Getty Images
(front), iStock/Gary Tognoni (back)
Casewrap: Jack Flash/Getty Images

Daici Ano for Nendo: 51, 52–53, 54, 55
Ryan Ballard: 106, 108, 109
Build LLC: 84
Layla Coats: 26, 28–29
Thomas Dukich: 76
Paige Eden Photography, Inc: 56, 58, 59
Elephant Room Creative: 31, 32, 33
Lili Engelhardt: 43, 44, 45
Rudy Hellmann Photography: 90
Deborah Hernandez: 95
Joseph Hopps: 93, 94
iStock/3DMaster: 8–9
iStock/Ken Wiedemann: 4–5
iStock/Willowpix: 142–143
Sevi Kocak: 14–15

Amadeus Leitner: 48, 49, 61, 62, 63, 64, 66, 67, 82, 83,
99, 100, 101, 110, 113, 119, 120, 121, 132, cover
(lower right)
Loll Designs: 69, 70, 71
London Fieldworks: 38, 40, 41, cover (upper right)
John Looser: 87, 88, 89
Dave and Steve Maslowski: 6, 7, 10, 11, 19, 46, 122, 128,
131, 133, 140, 144, cover (upper left)
Leo Matkins: 22
Michael Melford/Getty Images: 137
Wes Milholen: 112
Nature Society of Griggsville: 124, 125
Heiner Orth: 96
Ray Richardson Photography: 24, 25
Karel Roelofs: 72, 74, 75
Sami Sarkis/Getty Images: 16
J Schatz: 102, 104, 105, cover (lower left)
Courtesy SKYWALKER PROPERTIES, LTD: 20, 23
Jerry B. Smith Photograpy: 35, 36, 37
Brian Stewart–coxon/Dreamstime.com: 17
Alexander Studentschnig/Dreamstime.com: 134
Svetlana Tikhonova/Dreamstime.com: 13
Mary Vogel Photography: 114, 116, 117
Thomas Dambo Winther: 79, 80, 81, back cover

BIBLIOGRAPHY

Ehrlich, Paul R. *The Birdwatcher's Handbook*.
    Oxford University Press, 1994.

Garisto, Leslie. *The New Birdhouse Book*. Crestline, 1992.

Kaufman, Kenn. *Birds of North America* (Kaufman
    Focus Guides). Houghton Mifflin Harcourt, 2000.

Rael, Ronald. *Earth Architecture*.
    Princeton Architectural Press, 2008.

Sibley, David Allen. *The Sibley Guide to Birds*.
    Alfred A. Knopf, 2000.

Stokes, Donald and Lillian. *Stokes Birdhouse Book:
    The Complete Guide to Attracting Nesting
    Birds*. Little, Brown and Company, 1990.

Wade, J. L. *Attracting Purple Martins*. The Nature
    Society, 1987.

Wade, J. L. *What you should know About the
    Purple Martin: America's Most Wanted Bird*.
    Self-published, 1993.

Turkish Cultural Foundation,
    www.turkishculturalfoundation.org

North American Bluebird Society,
    www.nabluebirdsociety.org

Martha Stewart Cantitoe Corners House information
    sources: *New York Times* article, September 10,
    2006; *Martha Moments* blog,
    www.marthamoments.blog;
    The Martha Blog, themarthablog.com

Cornell Lab of Ornithology, www.birds.cornell.edu

The Nature Society, the purple martin organization
    founded in 1962, www.naturehouseinc.com

Big Picture Agriculture blog, produced by
    Kay McDonald, www.bigpictureagriculture.com

Wild Birds Unlimited, www.wbu.com

ACKNOWLEDGMENTS

This book would not have been possible without the help of many people. First and foremost I need to thank the makers of the birdhouses featured and the photographers who captured the essence of their creations. Without exception they have been generous and enthusiastic about the project. What a fine group of people. There seems to be a common thread of creativity, gentleness, decency, and fairness that runs through folks who love birdhouses and nature. A special shout out to Amadeus Leitner, a New Mexican photographer who made my life easier by taking many of the fabulous photographs highlighted in this book. He is a real pro. I also need to thank the fine nature and wildlife photographers Steve and Dave Maslowski for their fine photographs and for Steve's advice along the way. Liz Dineen, owner of Mariposa Gallery in Albuquerque and her gallery manager, George Brugnone, let me take over their space for a photo shoot and were generous and helpful to me the whole time.

I also want to thank my customers at Wild Birds Unlimited in St. Paul, Minnesota, and Santa Fe, New Mexico, for teaching me so much about birds and the people who love them. Thanks should also go to the staff at my store, who have picked up the slack for me as I've become immersed in the world of birdhouses.

My wonderful agent Meredith Bernstein worked hard on my behalf and was encouraging at every step.

All the top-notch professionals at my publisher Abrams deserve the credit for crafting this book and making it beautiful. They include my editors, Andrea Danese and Jennifer Levesque, for their fine work—Andrea guided me and this project through to the end with persistence and much skill. It would most certainly not be the book that it is without her. Danny Maloney helped me understand what makes a quality photograph; designer LeAnna Weller Smith made the book look great and managing editor Emily Albarillo helped with so many details and was very patient with me. Ivy McFadden provided excellent copyediting.

The folks at the Wild Birds Unlimited franchise office helped me anytime I had a question about birdhouses or the hobby of backyard birding. They are a competent and hard-working group and, as a Wild Birds Unlimited store owner, I am proud to be a part of their tribe. I especially want to thank Jim Carpenter, the founder, CEO, and president of Wild Birds Unlimited, who graciously gave me permission to use photographs and the nesting chart created by John Schaust and Brian Cunningham. I considered many different nesting charts and listings and theirs was by far my favorite.

Jeanne Schall came to my house many, many times to help me figure out a variety of computer and photography issues. She never one time made me feel stupid.

I appreciate the support of my sisters and former writing partners, Mary Schmauss and Geni Krolick. Mostly, I want to thank my partner Dawn Graber and our daughter, Mary, who listened patiently to my endless birdhouse stories. They urged me to take on this project and never complained when I became obsessed with it and stopped making dinner for them.

OPPOSITE: THIS MALE RED-SHAFTED NORTHERN FLICKER ATTENDS TO HUNGRY NESTLINGS IN ITS NEST, WHICH WAS MADE THE NATURAL WAY.

Published in 2014 by Stewart, Tabori & Chang
An imprint of ABRAMS

Library of Congress Control Number: 2013945635

ISBN: 978-1-61769-064-8

Editor: Andrea Danese
Designer: LeAnna Weller Smith
Production Manager: Tina Cameron

The text of this book was composed in Anandala, Avenir,
Blanch, Homestead, and Trend Sans.

Printed and bound in U.S.A.

10 9 8 7 6 5 4 3 2 1

Stewart, Tabori & Chang books are available at special
discounts when purchased in quantity for premiums and
promotions as well as fundraising or educational use. Special
editions can also be created to specification. For details,
contact specialsales@abramsbooks.com or the address below.

THE ART OF BOOKS SINCE 1949

115 West 18th Street
New York, NY 10011
www.abramsbooks.com

PREVIOUS SPREAD: A RUSTIC
WOODEN BIRDHOUSE AT
MONTEZUMA NATIONAL
WILDLIFE REFUGE IN WESTERN
NEW YORK.

BELOW: A RED-BELLIED
WOODPECKER AT ITS NEST,
A CAVITY INSIDE A TREE.